Exploring The Base Of Family Therapy

Exploring the Base for
Family Therapy

**Papers from the
M. Robert Gomberg
Memorial Conference**

Edited by

Nathan W. Ackerman, M.D.
Frances L. Beatman
Sanford N. Sherman

To the memory of

M. Robert Gomberg

1914–1958

Foreword

Dr. M. Robert Gomberg was executive director of Jewish Family Service of New York from 1949 until his untimely death in 1958. To honor him for his warm, vital leadership and for his creative contribution to family theory and family casework, an interdisciplinary conference was held on June 2 and 3, 1960, at the Academy of Medicine, New York, N. Y. At this conference a number of papers on theoretical and practical developments in family diagnosis, treatment, and research were presented by representatives of social work, psychiatry, and the social sciences

The choice of the family as subject, the convocation of representatives from different fields, and the range of contributions covering the specific and practical as well as the general and philosophical all represent appropriate testimonials to Dr. Gomberg. His professional career was characterized by an abiding interest in the family, by interdisciplinary interests, and by the catholicity of his approach.

In his personal life Dr. Gomberg was in essence a "family man." He accomplished the difficult feat of carrying a deeply personal role in his immediate family as well as in his extended family and, at the same time, a leadership role in his profession, without sacrificing one to the other. It was apparent to his colleagues and friends that his interest in family theory and his inveterate optimism about the durability of the family were in a large measure a reflection of his warm, rich, personal experiences in his family life.

Dr. Gomberg's capacity to respond sensitively to people was combined with unusual intellectual gifts. He was not only an intuitive technician but a scholar and philosopher. He had a distinguished career as practitioner, teacher, lecturer, and writer. He was deeply committed to the expansion of professional knowledge and skill through experimentation and research.

Shortly after his death on April 24, 1958, which occurred only an hour after he had delivered an address to the Eastern States Health Education Conference, a group of his associates constituted themselves the M. Robert Gomberg Memorial Committee. A Memorial

Fund was established to which a large number of his colleagues and friends contributed. The first tribute to Dr. Gomberg's memory, planned by the Committee and made possible by the Fund, was the Conference held in June, 1960. This volume is a compilation of the papers presented at that meeting. Since these papers constitute an important addition to the literature on the family, this volume represents a fitting memorial to Dr. Gomberg.

Thanks are extended to the members of the Memorial Committee: Dr. Nathan W. Ackerman, Arnold S. Askin, Frances L. Beatman, Irving Brodsky, Pauline B. Falk, Cora Kasius, Dr. Joseph P. Michelson, David Sher, and Sanford N. Sherman. Appreciation is also extended to the many donors to the Fund, to the editors of this volume, and to the Family Service Association of America which is serving as publisher.

PAULINE B. FALK
President, Board of Directors
Jewish Family Service
New York, New York

March 1, 1961

Contributors

Nathan W. Ackerman, M.D., Associate Clinical Professor of Psychiatry, Columbia University; Supervising and Research Psychiatrist, Family Mental Health Clinic, Jewish Family Service, New York; Chairman, Board of Directors, Family Institute, Inc., New York

Gregory Bateson, Ethnologist, Veterans Administration Hospital, Palo Alto, California

Frances L. Beatman, Executive Director, Jewish Family Service, New York

Marjorie L. Behrens, Research Associate, Central Research Unit, Jewish Board of Guardians, New York

Leonard S. Cottrell, Jr., Ph D., Social Psychologist and Secretary, Russell Sage Foundation, New York

Iago Galdston, M.D., Executive Secretary, Committee on Special Studies, New York Academy of Medicine

Don D. Jackson, M D., Director, Mental Research Institute, Palo Alto Medical Research Foundation; Chief, Department of Psychiatry, Palo Alto Medical Clinic

Weston LaBarre, Ph.D., Professor of Anthropology, Duke University, Durham, North Carolina

Hope J. Leichter, Ph.D., Director of Research Institute in Family Relations, Jewish Family Service, New York; Project Director, Russell Sage Foundation

Henry L. Lennard, Ph.D., Research Associate, Bureau of Applied Social Research, Columbia University; Social Science Consultant, Family Mental Health Clinic, Jewish Family Service, New York

Celia Mitchell, Chief Psychiatric Caseworker, Family Mental Health Clinic, Jewish Family Service, New York

Virginia Satir, Director of Training, Mental Research Institute, Palo Alto Medical Research Foundation

Sanford N. Sherman, Associate Executive Director, Jewish Family Service, New York

Lyman C. Wynne, M.D., Ph.D., Chief, Family Studies Section, Adult Psychiatry Branch, Clinical Investigations, National Institute of Mental Health, Bethesda, Maryland

Contents

Introduction 1

The Biosocial Unity of the Family....................... 5
Weston LaBarre

The Concept of the Family in Casework Therapy.......... 14
Sanford N. Sherman

A Review of Psychiatric Developments in Family Diagnosis
and Therapy...................................... 29
Don D. Jackson and *Virginia Satir*

A Dynamic Frame for the Clinical Approach to Family
Conflict 52
Nathan W. Ackerman

A Casework Approach to Disturbed Families............. 68
Celia Mitchell

Trends Toward Preventive Practice in Family Service....... 83
Frances L. Beatman

The Study of Intrafamilial Alignments and Splits in Exploratory Family Therapy............ 95
Lyman C. Wynne

The Biosocial Integration of Behavior in the Schizophrenic
Family 116
Gregory Bateson

The Need for an Epidemiology of Psychiatric Disorders of the
Family 123
Iago Galdston

CONTENTS

The Challenge of Research in Family Diagnosis and Therapy

Summary of Panel Discussion.....   135
                   Marjorie L. Behrens

  I. Formal Research in Family Structure..............   136
                   Gregory Bateson

  II. Boundaries of the Family as an Empirical and Theo-
     retical Unit   140
                   Hope J. Leichter

 III. Analysis of Family Conflict.......................   145
                   Henry L. Lennard

 IV. Interpersonal Competence and Preventive Mental
     Health   151
                 Leonard S. Cottrell, Jr.

Index   155

Introduction

THIS VOLUME is presented with the hope that it will be a useful addition to the steadily increasing fund of knowledge about family dynamics and family interactions. As the title indicates, the emphasis is on the exploration of theory about family processes as a foundation for treatment. The purpose of the M. Robert Gomberg Memorial Conference was to provide an opportunity for representatives of various disciplines working on family theory to exchange ideas and to report on research undertakings.

The value of such an exploration of theory, obviously, is to provide a conceptual base for family therapy. We are using the term "family therapy" in a broad, rather than a narrow, sense. We intend it to include various methods of treating and preventing family pathology as well as services designed to heighten the potential of the family to foster the well-being and mental health of its members.

Historically, the family has been the major focus of social work concern even though, on an organizational level, services have often been segmented. Emphasis on the family has been especially prominent in the evolution of the casework method, and was maintained as casework passed successively through periods of incorporating knowledge from sociology, psychology, and psychoanalysis. The techniques and methods of extending help, as well as the diagnostic base, went through radical revisions from time to time, but the aim of protecting and strengthening families has not swerved.

The historical trends in family casework have been reflected in the program of the Jewish Family Service of New York. In recent years, our agency, as well as many others, has been engaged in extending knowledge about family processes, drawing on new sociocultural theory. Various new approaches in treatment procedures, including family interviewing, have been introduced.

In relation to this volume, the agency's decision to inaugurate a family clinic, to supplement its family casework program, is of

1

particular significance. The Family Mental Health Clinic, which was established in 1956, serves as a means of linking casework and psychiatric efforts to investigate concepts of family diagnosis and therapy. In the clinic, sixty families are currently under treatment. Family group interviewing is the most common modality. The written records of these interviews, together with an already extensive library of sound films of family group-therapy sessions, form the raw data for study. Approaches to making systematic family diagnoses are being explored; various ways of classifying and integrating data are being investigated for the ultimate purpose of developing family typologies; and the dynamics of family therapy and the changes that occur under therapy are being identified. In short, the clinic is engaged in a process of theory building about the nature of family processes, about the connections between individual and family mental health, and about the effects of therapeutic intervention.

Throughout the country a number of clinics, institutes, and departments of hospitals and universities are working in a parallel fashion with similar goals. Among such centers of practical experiment and research are those affiliated with the University of Chicago, Harvard University, and Yale University; the Mental Research Institute in Palo Alto, California; and the National Institute of Mental Health in Bethesda, Maryland. Outstanding persons in the fields of psychoanalysis, psychiatry, casework, and the social sciences are engaged in these ventures.

The extensive quest for family theory has doubtless been motivated by the fact that the helping professions have often reached a *cul de sac* in the treatment of individual social maladaptation, emotional disturbance, and mental illness. The preoccupation with individual psychic processes which has characterized helping efforts during the past few decades unquestionably brought great advances in psychological theory as well as in therapeutic procedures but these individual-oriented techniques have not always accomplished the desired ends. It has become increasingly clear that a major break-through in theory is necessary if substantial further advances are to be made. Such a break-through would seem to lie in the direction of the conceptual synthesis of psychological and social determinants of behavior, a synthesis to be found in family theory.

2

The family is the primary biosocial unit in our culture. The study of integration of individual behavior within the family, therefore, is the major task facing the helping professions. Such study will need to include processes within the family as well as the family's relations with the larger community. Each family member influences family processes and the family, in turn, molds individual behavior. Because the decisive transactions that take place within the family are multiple and complex, present efforts to identify and classify the phenomena can be considered only preliminary forays.

This collection of papers, therefore, represents one contribution to the total effort of theory building about family processes. The reports of experimental clinical procedures and of tentative research findings excite the imagination and buttress the growing conviction that family therapy holds great promise. The more clearly we see that the individual's mental health is linked, in subtle ways, with what takes place within the family, the more convinced we become of the value of therapeutic intervention in family processes. Such intervention may sometimes be the best way to treat a disturbed individual and it may often be a necessary concomitant to individual treatment.

The many recent contributions to family theory are the result of the foresight and inventiveness of the many individuals and teams of individuals engaged in research or in clinical practice. Certain societal developments, however, have unquestionably created a culture favorable to the acceleration of such study of the family. The rapid sociocultural changes of the past few decades have brought about the alteration of many social institutions and processes. Nowhere is the alteration more evident than in the structure and internal life of the American family. Many research investigators are currently endeavoring to identify these changes, and to study the relationships between the changes in the family and the social behavior and psychic stability of the individual.

It seems likely that the instability of the American family has stimulated certain processes of social control in the larger society, one of which is the pursuit of scientific understanding of family dynamics. Such advances in knowledge should further the development of measures that will check the corrosive influences on the family and strengthen the stabilizing ones. Advances in knowledge hold promise for the enrichment of family life and, therefore, for the enrichment of the lives of its members.

NATHAN W. ACKERMAN, M.D.
FRANCES L. BEATMAN
SANFORD N. SHERMAN
Editors

The Biosocial Unity of the Family

Weston LaBarre

A WHOLE GENERATION of anthropologists has been busy at a task that we can say is now well accomplished. This task was to break down the naive ethnocentrism and cultural absolutism existing in all un-self-examined societies, including our own. In some sectors of our society this tribal fundamentalism admittedly still remains, but most literate and informed persons are now aware of the fact of cultural relativity. In its consequences this relativity may yet be as revolutionary in our thinking as Einstein's discovery of relativity in mathematical physics—and may even help in some degree to rescue us from the worst consequences of this physical discovery. Perhaps the discovery of cultural relativism is a salvation and a necessity in a world now grown small through man's communications, for it shows us a new freedom and responsibility to modify the clashes between culture and culture, and it gives us a necessary humility as we set about our major contemporary moral task in history.

In some ways, this discovery of cultural relativism was also intellectually necessary. For instance, psychology puts forward many generalizations concerning universal human nature which are clearly no more than local folklore. Thus Kinsey unwittingly came upon contemporary American superstitions about sexuality, for example the superstition that males are oversexed and females undersexed. He did not, as he thought, discover universally

5

valid facts about human males and females. It is easy for the anthropologist, armed with comparative evidence, to trip up these would-be psychological absolutists; that is, the comparative method of anthropology, which Kinsey did not use, stands ready and willing to rescue the behavioral sciences from propounding folklore.

Recognition of Cultural Relativism

It is desirable that a wide and informed public recognize the cultural relativism of our economic and political systems, for otherwise we would not be motivated to criticize our inherited social institutions for the human constructs they are, or to revise and plan new institutions intelligently, or to select sound aspects of the old that we would wish to defend. In this we are only rediscovering the wisdom of the Old Testament prophets, which has profoundly influenced our Judeo-Christian tradition. The prophets knew that man's ways are not those of God, that cultures are not the same as the objective that-which-is, and that a better future can be assured by reforming man's ways more in conformity with that objective reality. Like the Greeks, we have now widely discovered the difference between the given physical universe *(physis)* and man-made custom *(nomos)*, and this is a valuable discovery. Indeed, this Judeo-Greek willingness to accept the feedback of experience is at the very base of science, a development historically unique to scientific tradition. The willingness of the prophets to criticize contemporary mores is of a piece with the willingness of the scientist to criticize contemporary theories.

The high point of modern cultural relativity in America was probably reached in Ruth Benedict's famous book, *Patterns of Culture.*[1] Here culture A and cultures B and C are put side by side comparatively, in vividly contrastive circumstantial detail. But it is all too easy, in the use of this passively comparative method, to collapse into a feckless and shapeless moral relativism—to suppose that culture A is "as good as" culture B, and B as C, and to conclude that "it is all relative anyway." Moreover, this kind of relativ-

[1] Ruth Benedict, *Patterns of Culture,* Houghton Mifflin Co., Boston, 1934

ism is constantly used to rationalize a disloyalty to some currently irksome moral demand. And so we throw the baby (man) out with the bathwater (culture).

It is true that in the last analysis all cultures are based on moral stances. But we forget that moralities are adapative—that cultures are differentially adaptive, and that some culture traits are more adaptive than others. How else can we explain the historical fact that cultures rise and fall and that some cultures even disappear in time? Cultural traits are adapative, not as we think they are, but as they are historically, differentially and in hard biological fact. Culturally, man proposes; historically, reality disposes. It is correct to say that all races are equally capable of propounding cultures, but it is incorrect to suppose from this that all the cultures propounded are therefore equally adaptive. We talk as if man were some kind of Existentialist spider, spinning culture and a web of symbolism out of his own wishful body-substances—and then walking on it over the void Perhaps we humans in fact do this. Perhaps we do embroider all kinds of fanciful alternative patterns in the center of the web. But we must not forget that the guywires of the web must be attached to natural reality somewhere, soundly and adaptively, if we are to walk on the web with any safety.

Cultural relativity as a concept can therefore be pressed too far. Sometimes, indeed, we mistake for contingent culture certain behaviors that are actually part of our universal human biology. One of these biological systems, and one quite unassailable by cultural relativity, is the human family. One may ring all the changes he likes on the varying cultural forms of the family, but the biological fact remains that all human societies have the nuclear family of father, mother, and children—plus or minus additional but separable characteristics involving structure, economics, adult authority, and the like. It is all very well for Malinowski [2] to show us that in the Trobriand Islands some of the economic and disciplinary functions of the father are held by another male adult, the mother's brother, but the adult economic and disciplinary functions toward children are still there. To be sure, the Trobrianders may have a kind of Oedipus complex different from ours—indeed they must

[2] Bronislav Malinowski, *Sex and Repression in Savage Society,* Harcourt, Brace and Co., New York, 1927.

7

have, since the family form is different—but the family is still there. Until Trobrianders marry their mothers we shall continue to believe that the nuclear family is a human universal, not culturally contingent but biologically fundamental.

Man as a Mammal

It is important for practical persons attempting therapy, such as family caseworkers, and for responsible citizens on agency planning boards to know the sound foundations of their professional efforts. We are not weaving on the wind when we work in terms of the family; we are merely trying to make a fundamental human institution more usefully and healthily adaptive.

The family is not only universal among all groups of man, it is also unique to man. That is, the family is specifically a human-biological dispensation. In the casual nature-faking of stories told to children, we too easily, and falsely, impute human social organization and the family to other animals. There is, we are told, a Mister Michael Mouse, apparently interminably engaged to a Miss Minerva Mouse—but the simple fact is that mice do not have engagement periods, long or short! Again, there is a Mister Donald Duck who, we are given to understand, has three duckling nephews —but the literal fact is the ducks just don't have nephews!

The old-fashioned mammalian family is made up only of the mother and her offspring, as in bears or in seals. The sexes breed seasonally and then separate; the mother-child "family" based on lactation lasts only a brief time, then mother and offspring separate. Mammary glands are the most ancient trait in mammals, for we find them already in the duck-billed platypus which still lays eggs The non-seasonal, year-round sexual drive that keeps the sexes permanently together is a far later mammalian trait, which first appeared, we understand, in the tree-living primates, the monkey and anthropoid ape cousins of man. Man is not a second-rate, decadent mammal at all, as many people have tried to maintain. Man is the most mammalian of all the mammals.

One mammalian trait, for example, is maternal care of the young. In maternal care the human female is the most exuberantly mammalian of all the mammals. The permanent breast, as opposed to

8

reappearing animal teats, is found only in the human female mammal and in man's own milch animals, such as cows, domesticated long after humans acquired this characteristic and after the same pattern. (It is biologically unjust to call a woman a "cow"; in the evolutionary sense one could only call a cow a "woman"!) Another trait of mammals is the protracted care of the young, in which the human female performs extravagant prodigies. Such care lasts not for a season or two, but often for decades. Still another mammalian trait is the dependency of the young. Human infants are as helpless as mammalian infants can be, and they certainly protract their dependent infancy for a far longer period in time than any other mammal. Some of our very human racial traits are based on a kind of differential and permanent human infantilization. For example, all human babies are born with "button noses," but Mongoloids like the Chinese may retain the button nose as a lifelong racial trait.

Thus, just as the human physique is modified in the permanent breast within the domestications of the family, as well as in the physiological change from seasonal oestrus or "heat" to near-permanent cyclic menstruation, so also the biological pattern of family living has structured the physiques of humans radically. Let us not forget that the human male is also a high-order mammal. In terms of year-round, non-seasonal sexual interest in the human female, and the consequently near-permanent protection of her and her young, the human male is obviously the best mammal in the business! The human father, to put it another way, has come home to stay—for whatever advantages and dire consequences and complications this entails. In humans alone is found the fully social and moral father, contrasted with the merely procreative male in other mammals. The uniquely human family, we must insist, forms the very basis of our unique humanity. The nature of human nature is that of a family living animal.

The longer period of pregnancy in humans, coupled with the greatly longer period of dependency and protection which secures a much higher rate of survival in the young, makes it plainly evident that human mammals do not need the extra sexual bonds for purely *procreative* purposes. Human sexuality clearly serves *social* purposes in this new biosocial unit, the human family.

9

Father comes home to stay, not for dreary and diverse and contingent cultural reasons, but because, biologically speaking, he wants to.

We need to forget the false animal fables about ducks and mice, and recognize that the family represents a new kind of biological unit rather than the solitary, only seasonally sexual, wild-animal individual organism, adapting through its instincts and its genes to its environment. For interindividually shared culture is man's primary adaptation to nature biologically, and human culture is impossible without the family matrix to transmit it. Indeed, our entire social humanity derives from the human family. Thus, we are not so much instinctual animals, born full-panoplied with instincts that will soon enable us to adapt inflexibly and automatically to the environment as self-sufficient adults. Instead, we are learning animals, with big brains, adapted to borrowing most of our adaptations from other animals of our species, associated with us for biological reasons during our long individual dependency. We build our nature on our nurture. We build our culture on our sociability; and, in an even more minute sense, the specific family we live in is the laboratory of personality in the individual. We learn our very humanity, we are taught how to be human in terms of our tribe, we develop our individual personalities—all primarily and first within the family.

Thus it is that any pathology in a family may result in a fundamental mislearning by the child in the family. Every neurosis is taught and learned; hence the very fact of being human offers the possibility of being neurotic. Again, language, that fantastic web of symbols and human interindividuality that has no objective status whatever in non-human reality, has grown up only in our intensely social human species. Even the dance "language" of bees, which tells the distance and direction of honey-bearing flowers, could have grown up only in a species of social insects. Other social animals, such as monkeys, have emotion-stating cries, which announce the subjective state of the animal for various adaptive purposes, such as fleeing a common enemy, frightening off other monkeys from the feeding territory, or for love-making. But only human beings have authentic language through which they can discriminatingly point to objective situations in the universe out-

10

side themselves. All humans have one kind or another of language—and only human beings have language. The same is true, by and large, of culture, for which langage is the major vehicle. Other animals, like monkeys, have imitative fads, but only humans have languages and traditional social cultures. Symbol-systems like language would be only feeble nonce-structures—private "familiar" understandings born with and perishing with each family—were it not that the universal human incest taboo forces a circulation of individuals from old to new families, and thus makes common social coinage of private-familial symbol systems. That is, only human sociosexual structure (nuclear families within larger societies) makes any of these languages or cultures possible.

The Social Institutions of Man

The family is the ultimate source of all our human institutions. Morality itself has had its birth in the family, when first the human father ceases to kill his offspring as his rivals for the mother—as stallions kill their own colts, male bears their own biological cubs, and buck rabbits their bunny offspring. Abraham became quite truly "Father Abraham," and symbolic father of all humanity, when he listened to the voice of morality and refrained from killing Isaac. This is the biological bargain on which the human family is founded: the father must permit the infant care of his young and their years-long dependency on the mother, in order for human nurture to operate; and by the same bargain, no male infant may be the procreative rival of his father for his own mother in the same family. This is the categorical imperative, the absolutely universal and uniquely human incest taboo, non-existent in any other animal.

Every human individual must leave the family of origin, in which his biological business is that of the child, maturing physically into the adult animal and psychologically into a human being, and learning his humanity in the biosocial terms that are given him. Then, grown mature, every human being, if he will, must forge his own specific family of procreation, in which his biological business is now that of an adult, to provide security for the infantile members of his species. Of course, there are many

11

sublimations of this basic human drive, but the hallmark of adulthood in every case is responsibility for other members of our species. Thus, the family is the forum of all human morality, and grows out of the biologically built-in, intensely interindividual bonds of male and female and of mother and child. Culture so often forces repression and modification of these drives that we sometimes forget their overwhelming intensity. Our humanity itself is based on the intense interindividuality of human biosocial bonds.

Our other social institutions are uniformly based on the family as well. When men form societies larger than the family, they customarily borrow the pattern of the family to form purely ritual "blood-brotherhoods" through magic initiation ceremonies that make members tribal "brothers" of one another, the larger fraternity being a pseudo-family moral ingroup, as if this were the best and only way to form societies. And we can still usefully speak of "the brotherhood of man," still not sufficiently realized, as a further way of humanizing ourselves. The state itself as a sociolegal institution represents our endless search for fatherly authority that promises sibling equality before this authority. The religions man contrives inveterately borrow the language of the family, and rightly so, for in them do we not seek a divine father and his moral authority and make our peace with a family-nurtured conscience? So, too, with all our other social institutions; they are all, I believe, ultimately founded on the mystique of the human family. The end result is the kind of human animal that through evolution we have built ourselves to be.

Thus it is that in such an institution as social casework in its various agencies we are always soundly attempting to build upon the family. When the family fails to perform its necessary functions we must seek other social means to take up the slack, such as child welfare and old age social security. When misgrowths occur in sick or pathological families, we have to provide re-growth and re-learning, through psychiatric, casework, and group therapy. Indeed, all therapy is in a sense group therapy, involving always a reconstruction of relationships in that basic group, the family. As for the theoretical bases of our practical work, once we have seen clearly into the nature of human nature, we need have no further worry

12

or concern. Ours is no "reactionary" doomed attempt to shore up a decadent "bourgeois" or "democratico-capitalistic" failing institution. It is rather an attempt to help other human beings to find how best to realize their own humanity, as it is biologically given to us in this animal species. Through all its cultural relativisms —and these are sometimes alarmingly wide indeed—the nuclear human family persists, perennially, for it is based in our fundamental human biology, in our nature as universally and uniquely family-living animals.

The Concept of the Family in Casework Theory

Sanford N. Sherman

IN RECENT YEARS, social role theory has been found useful in the diagnosis and treatment of the individual family, and in various types of research on the family as a social unit. The comprehensive Curriculum Study of the Council on Social Work Education proposes the concept of social role as a cornerstone of social casework theory.[1] Since this proposition is receiving much attention in the field, it may be interesting to go back almost two decades when caseworkers seemed to be thinking of the family only as the backdrop against which to view the individual client. In 1944, Dr. Gomberg wrote:

> . . . when family casework accepts as its focus a responsibility to the whole family, it defines a useful uniformity of purpose, structure, and method in spite of the large variety of problems and services with which it deals. This responsibility includes an understanding of family *organization and the different roles* [my italics] normally assumed by the several members of a family . . . [and helping] the client or clients to re-establish or preserve their different roles within the family.[2]

I should like to point out four implications of Dr. Gomberg's statement: (1) social role adaptation is proposed as a construct, by means of which (2) separate perceptions of the emotional, biological, social, and cultural forces shaping behavior can be integrated, and

---

[1] Werner W. Boehm, *The Social Casework Method in Social Work*, (Vol. X, Social Work Curriculum Study), Council on Social Work Education, New York, 1959.
[2] M. Robert Gomberg, "The Specific Nature of Family Case Work," in *A Functional Approach to Family Case Work*, Jessie Taft (ed), University of Pennsylvania Press, Philadelphia, 1944, p. 147.

14

(3) some systematic order can be brought to an understanding of a multitude of individual and family variables, so that (4) family and individual distress can be evaluated and treated. This formulation is extraordinarily similar to the propositions of Werner Boehm and others, which now are looked upon as "new thinking" in the field. In the brief history of social work theory, a period of sixteen years is a millennium, and this fact adds impressiveness to Dr. Gomberg's contribution.

Of a large number of concepts that are useful in analyzing the family as a functioning organism, I have selected for discussion social role theory and several others that I believe are particularly relevant to the issues in social casework today.

Social casework, as is generally known, had its origins in a primarily social and sociological approach to individual and family problems. Following World War I, social caseworkers became increasingly vexed by the discrepancies they found between objective facts and the subjective experiences of their clients. In their efforts to understand these inconsistencies, they turned first to psychological and then to psychiatric and psychoanalytic concepts through which their practice could be enriched. By the 1930's, the "sophisticated" social work model of personality was bio-psychic and had lost its earlier sociological character. When an individual was in trouble and needed help, the caseworker had to assess the "inner and outer" stresses influencing his behavior, and decide which were etiologically more prominent and more susceptible to change. In casework thinking, inner and outer stresses were clearly separated. By 1940, however, caseworkers were beginning to express their concern that focusing on the emotional condition of the client had resulted in subordinating and neutralizing their understanding of social factors.

Family as the Key to the Psychosocial Riddle

This dichotomy has persisted, however, and the past twenty years have been marked by many restatements of it.[3] Attempts at

---

[3] Elizabeth G Meier, "Social and Cultural Factors in Casework Diagnosis," *Social Work*, Vol. IV, No. 3 (1959), pp. 15–26.

uniting these two elements led to the emergence in the casework lexicon of the term "psychosocial" which reflected an awareness, but on a high level of abstraction, of the unity of personality.

Thus, Gordon Hamilton stated in 1941 that "in the first exposure to psychiatry one thought of the 'emotional' problem, mistakenly called 'the real problem,' as something behind or underneath the social problem, instead of grasping the fact that problems to one degree or another are psychosocial." "Only diagnostic ability," she proceeded to state, "can distinguish those maladjustments which arise chiefly from economic and cultural factors and those with more complicated psychosocial causality." [4]

Casework theory has been making only small advances in resolving this problem. Whether one searches the professional literature or observes casework practice, a critical eye can discern the gap that exists between theory on a high level which is organismic in orientation and emphasizes psychosocial integration, and the actual analysis, diagnosis, and treatment of specific cases which deal almost exclusively with emotional aspects of personality and personality maladjustment.[5] In theory, caseworkers affirm the importance of social and cultural influences on the client's personality and his problem; but in practice they find it difficult to use their knowledge of these influences, except peripherally. In characteristic fashion, caseworkers have taken one of two opposing courses in trying to resolve this dilemma. Either they look upon other than emotional factors as incidental and ancillary, or they suggest— especially with reference to the socially disorganized and depressed, or "hard-core" family—that a kind of social therapy be attempted without reference to clinical skills.

There have been encouraging reports of various attempts to bridge this long-standing gap. On the practice level, Regensburg has reported the use of concepts of family equilibrium in the work

---

[4] Gordon Hamilton, "The Underlying Philosophy of Social Case Work," *The Family*, Vol. XXII, No. 5 (1941), p. 141.

[5] See Sidney J. Berkowitz, "Some Specific Techniques of Psychosocial Diagnosis and Treatment in Family Casework," *Social Casework*, Vol. XXXVI, No. 9 (1955), pp. 399–406; also Florence Hollis, "The Relationship Between Psychosocial Diagnosis and Treatment," *Social Casework*, Vol. XXXII, No. 2 (1951), pp. 67-74.

of the Community Service Society of New York.[6] Pollak has reported efforts in Pittsburgh and Philadelphia family agencies to use a family model as the basis for arriving at a diagnosis.[7] The New Orleans attempts to base family diagnosis on social science concepts of role interaction as well as on clinical indices have been reported by Weiss and Monroe.[8] The Jewish Family Service of New York has found Ackerman's contribution to be the most thoroughgoing and the most practicable in its attempts to integrate theory and practice, and the orientation of this paper can be credited, in large part, to the influence of his ideas.[9]

All those who have worked on problems of family theory and practice, whatever their individual differences, have in common two experiences. First, is the conviction that the family is a suitable anvil on which to forge the unity of the inner and outer (the psychic and the social) aspects of personality, and the unity of inner conflict and behavior disturbance; the process whereby the individual is integrated into the family system is bio-psycho-social in character. Second, is the agreement that much hard work and rumination are required to piece together in a single case, and incompletely at that, an evaluation that reflects the bio-psycho-social interplay that exists. As so often has been said, our concepts and tools are either inappropriate or inadequate.[10] We often find ourselves trying to fuse the familiar dynamic psychological concepts with those of social science, even though, from our vantage point as practitioners, social science concepts appear to be less specific or merely descriptive. If, however, the social science concepts are viewed as a point of departure, and the psychological

[6] Jeanette Regensburg, "Casework Diagnosis of Marital Problems—Application of Psychoanalytic Concepts," in *Neurotic Interaction in Marriage*, Victor W. Eisenstein (ed.), Basic Books, New York, 1956, pp. 244–261.

[7] Otto Pollak, "A Family Diagnosis Model," *Social Service Review*, Vol. XXXIV, No. 1 (1960), pp. 19–28.

[8] Viola Weiss and Russell R. Monroe, "A Framework for Understanding Family Dynamics," *Social Casework*, Vol. XL, Nos. 1 and 2 (1959), pp. 3–9; 80–87.

[9] Nathan W. Ackerman, *The Psychodynamics of Family Life*, Basic Books, New York, 1958.

[10] M Robert Gomberg, "Family Diagnosis: Trends in Theory and Practice," *Social Casework*, Vol. XXXIX, Nos. 2–3 (1958), pp. 73–83; Otto Pollak, "Family Diagnosis: Commentary," *Social Casework*, Vol. XXXIX, Nos. 2–3 (1958), pp. 83–85.

dimension is "built in," there can be considerable reward in the new insights gained.

The Family as a Whole

I suggested earlier that family theory can furnish one of the answers to the psychological riddle at this phase in the development of casework. Our expanding knowledge of ego psychology has revealed that psychic and emotional growth and the socialization of the child's individual personality are two sides of the same coin. The basic processes of socialization take place in the primary family group. Integration into peer groups, educational groups, and occupational groups follows. The adult continues the socialization process as he integrates his marital and parental roles in the conjugal family group. Thus, socialization is a continuous process of psychological and biological integration by the individual of his roles within various groups; and the family group is the primary and chronologically first group in this continuum.

It is obvious, therefore, that if we are to understand the individual, we must also understand the structure, function, and vital processes of the group as a discrete system. It is for this reason that, in this past decade, "family diagnosis" has been coming to the fore as a focus of interest, replacing an interest in "family-oriented" diagnosis. "Changing from family-oriented to *family* diagnosis and treatment is more than an increase in intensity of the same approach. It represents a shift to viewing the distress of the individual as less the problem than a symptom of the problem of pathology in the whole family." [11] Family diagnosis is oriented to "the client *in* the family" and their reciprocal interplay; it replaces the separatism expressed in the phrase "the client *and* his family." One cannot overemphasize the basic difference in orientation produced by the substitution of the word "in" for the word "and." The "in" orientation is holistic; the "and" orientation atomistic. These differing orientations reflect differences not only in personality theory but also in practical family analysis.

[11] Sanford N Sherman, "Joint Interviews in Casework Practice," *Social Work,* Vol. IV, No. 2 (1959), p. 21.

One approach is to comprehend and analyze the whole (the family) as a necessary concurrent condition to understanding or analyzing the part (the individual); the other approach defines components (individuals) and attempts to comprehend the whole (the family) by interrelation and synthesis. As Zimbalist points out, the first— the holistic or organismic orientation—is harmonious with social work tradition.[12] Relevant, too, are the comments of an unusually perceptive social worker of over twenty years ago. Ada Sheffield said that a segmental approach "makes a piecemeal advance toward understanding by viewing situation-items *atomistically,* and moving additively toward a grasp of the whole, whereas a psychosocial whole operates as a *system,* which like an organism conditions the very nature of its interdependent elements." [13]

Gomberg has documented the recent history of concepts of the family-as-a-whole in diagnosis and treatment.[14] It is clear that this history records a movement from separatism toward holism; from an operational approach to the family as a congeries of individuals to a view of the family as having an identity of its own; from a one-sided clinical approach to the individual to an encompassing of the individual and the family of which he is part. In short, it is a movement from family-*oriented* diagnosis and treatment to *family* diagnosis and treatment. This movement is a thread that runs through the literature of the period.

In an article written in 1941, Florence T. Waite pointed out that family casework had moved beyond the older emphasis on trying to know and be in touch with several family members.[15] It had developed a clinical orientation and tended to concentrate on the individual because: (1) competitiveness and jealousy existed among family members; (2) seeing the whole family blurred the autonomy of the individual and the worker was apt to take over the family too completely and overpoweringly; (3) society has increased its

[12] Sidney E. Zimbalist, "Organismic Social Work Versus Partialistic Research," *Social Casework,* Vol XXXIII, No. 1 (1952), p. 6.
[13] Ada Sheffield, *Social Insight in Case Situations,* Appleton-Century, New York, 1937, p. 256, as quoted by Zimbalist, *ibid.*
[14] M. Robert Gomberg, "Family Diagnosis: Trends in Theory and Practice," *op. cit.*
[15] Florence T. Waite, "Case Work—Today and Fifty Years Ago," *The Family,* Vol. XXI, No. 10 (1941), pp. 315–322.

emphasis on the individual even at the expense of his membership in the family and society at large. This point of view represents the prevailing apotheosis of the individual clinical approach.

By 1948, this positivist, individual-only approach was giving way, and almost a note of defensiveness is evidenced in this quotation from Regina Flesch:

> An individual's marriage is, after all, an expression of the individual's total personality. To the marital relationship, based upon early family experience, the individual brings his hopes, fears, and ability to love . . . marriage does not alter personal problems but simply provides a new avenue for their expression. The marital discord then is a symptom of other conflicts.[16]

A significant step forward was taken by Patricia Sacks who, in 1949, discussed the focus on the separate and unique individual problems of each marital partner, and the opposing view that "exaggeratedly suggests marriage is an entity itself, over and beyond the individuals united in it." [17] She concluded that it was "timely to consolidate the points of emphasis in these two approaches, each of which has some validity."

During subsequent years the literature has increasingly stressed the enhancement of individual diagnosis and treatment brought about by an orientation to family diagnosis and treatment. There has been continued movement toward the fuller appreciation of the individual's linkage with the conjugal pair, with the parent-child pair or triad, and with the entire family unit.

Individual Behavior as a Function of the Family Group

The zealousness shown in attempting to apply family theory to problems of casework practice has been hindered by the lack of adequate conceptual equipment. Social science theory holds great promise, but its essentially descriptive and general character seems to limit its integration with dynamic psychology. It can serve well, however, as the steel skeletal structure around which clinicians

---

[16] Regina Flesch, "Treatment Goals and Techniques in Marital Discord," *Social Casework*, Vol. XXIX, No. 10 (1948), p. 388.
[17] Patricia Sacks, "Establishing the Diagnosis in Marital Problems," *Social Casework*, Vol. XXX, No. 5 (1949), p. 182.

can fill in the masonry. There seems little doubt that those professions based on a dynamic psychology are moving closer to biosocial theory, while many social scientists who are working along-
side clinicians are developing a clinical orientation. Thus, *social*
casework is joined by *social* psychiatry and *social* psychology while,
on the other bank of the ever-narrowing moat, are the *clinical*
anthropologists, *clinical* sociologists, and so on. The research activities in which both clinical and social science workers are now
employed are too numerous to mention.

In connection with the problem of systematically analyzing whole
families, it has been said that "one must accept the fact that the
interactions among family members are so numerous that not all of
them can be understood and treated. Thus, a way must be found to
identify among a large number of interactions those that are crucial,
positively and negatively, for effective social functioning." [18]

This statement could well be paraphrased to apply to the problems of the clinician who confronts the infinite variety of vital
processes that go on simultaneously in one individual. Just as
clinical practice has found constructs and typologies for systematic
understanding and treatment of the individual, so there are now
being forged constructs for diagnosis and therapy of the family.
Kurt Lewin stated that behavior is a function of personality and
environment.[19] In the context of this paper, one could say that
behavior is a function of personality *and the family group.*

Homeostasis of the Family Group

A chief foundation stone for building the understanding of the
family as an interactional field is the concept of homeostasis.
Ackerman and Jackson, particularly, have illuminated this concept.[20] Borrowed from the physiological sciences, it gives coherent
meaning to the intricate pattern of transactional processes in the

---

[18] Werner W. Boehm, "The Social Work Curriculum Study and Its Implications for Family Casework," *Social Casework*, Vol. XL, No. 8 (1959), p. 435.

[19] Kurt Lewin, *A Dynamic Theory of Personality*, McGraw-Hill Publishing
Co., New York, 1960.

[20] Nathan W. Ackerman, *The Psychodynamics of Family Life, op. cit*; Don
D. Jackson, "The Question of Family Homeostasis," *Psychiatric Quarterly
Supplement*, Part I, Vol. XXXI, No. 1 (1957), pp. 79–90.

21

family. A life force operates in the family through alignments between individuals, joining of identities, complementation, and other processes. This force tends to equilibrate, stabilize, and continuously adapt and readapt family members to each other, and the family to its individuals, in the face of changes from within and from without. Josselyn has termed it a "steering mechanism." [21] Its effect is centripetal and gyroscopic and it is in actuality an adaptational process that maintains family equilibrium. Although homeostasis is a principle on a high level of generality, it serves as a necessary foundation for the development of more particularized concepts.

The particular ways in which a family maintains balance and adaptation are individual to that family; the pattern of adaptation and the maintenance of balance in each family can be viewed as the summation of all of the interpersonal and intrapersonal processes that occur in the family. In fact, when we succeed in developing family typologies, the most meaningful classifications will stem from the delineation of differences in family patterns of dynamic adaptation and equilibration rather than from the structural differences in families Viewing families in this way introduces the factor of time. One can determine how the family organism adapts and grows, maintains control or loses it, by analyzing the family as a structural and interactional entity at a certain point in time and then analyzing it as it was at important points of change or crisis, by moving backward in time to the family's origin in courtship and marriage. Just as a meaningful history illuminates our perception of an individual's current identity, conflicts, and adaptation, so the past history of a family illuminates our understanding of the family and of the individuals that comprise it.

Case Illustration

A case recently discussed in a seminar involved a young man, an average middle-class individual, who had developed a number of phobias, was anxious about his job performance, and so on.

[21] Irene M. Josselyn, "The Family as a Psychological Unit," *Social Casework*, Vol. XXXIV, No. 8 (1953), pp. 336–343.

The family caseworker had attempted to make a diagnostic assessment of this man, the marital pair, and the family. However, despite the many insights into the man's passivity, the marital relationship, and so on, the seminar group still felt that the situation was inadequately understood. For example, why did Mr. Black develop symptoms at this particular time? If these symptoms were primarily a response to his wife's recent extra-marital affairs, why had *she* begun to act out sexually after nine years of marriage? The often crucial question in therapy, "why at this particular time?" had to be answered in this case. The seminar group then plotted a time sequence of important internal and external events in this family's life, year by year. This ordering and juxtaposing of objective and subjective events in sequence resulted in the group's achieving an integration of fragments of understanding into a different whole. The recurrent influence on the family of Mrs. B's mother became clear, from the history. The extent of this influence could be discerned in the daughter's internal conflict, caused, in part, by an unresolved mother-daughter relationship, in the presence of the mother and her contemporary influence on Mrs. B, in the complementarity between Mrs. B and her husband, and in the control of conflict within the B family.

Mrs. B's sexual acting out had taken place immediately following her mother's death—an event that Mrs. B had mentioned only incidentally in a quite different connection. Mrs. B's mother had exerted a strong influence on her daughter's choice of Mr. B as a mate. Even though Mrs. B's mother had not lived with the B family, and had seen them infrequently, she had been an important ghostly presence in the B family. Her death had triggered Mrs. B's loss of control and a shift in the marital balance, and thereby had lowered Mr. B's threshold of defense against his dormant pathological anxiety. Understanding how the family's control system had broken down illuminated, in turn, certain aspects of the individual diagnoses. Mrs. B had come from a cultural and religious background in which personal sinfulness was considered to be innate and in which pleasurable impulses were denied and converted into moral and upright behavior. She was involved in a hostile but close relationship with a morally rigid,

23

essentially impersonal mother. Although she was distant from her father—a beaten man, a failure, but a sport—she was aligned and joined in some respects with him.

This woman's adolescent experiences bespoke her effort to carry out her mother's injunction to be on guard against sexual and other gratifications. She and her husband had been practically betrothed in middle adolescence. Mr. B was "safe," unvirile, and passive. These qualities were a buttress to Mrs. B's need to "play dead" and to keep in check her impulses toward having fun and pleasure. Before marriage, when Mr. B had been in the army, she had become enamored of another man who was, in many respects, the opposite of Mr. B. She reported that her "parents" (meaning, no doubt, her mother) had interfered and insisted on her remaining faithful to Mr. B. The conflict was between Mrs. B's desire for sexual excitement, gratification, fun, pleasure and living, which were "dangerous," and her wish for safety, repression, and deadness. The two sides of her conflict were externally represented, in part, by the characters of her father and mother, and also by her second suitor and Mr. B. She had only partially internalized her mother's influence in buttressing the denial, and her mother's continued existence had served as a warning presence. Both the mother and Mr. B, whom she had chosen as a son-in-law, had served to strengthen Mrs. B's defense of denial and to control her conflict.

The complementarity in this marriage was also evident. Just as Mr. B helped his wife to check her dormant adventurousness and maintain a pseudo-safety, so her interest in fun and pleasure and her role as social ambassador for the family stimulated pleasure-loving in him, and made him feel less isolated and more alive. This tenuous complementarity was tinged with pathology and was only partly successful. A chain reaction of breakdown in control had been set off by a seemingly irrelevant event. Just as Mr. B's ability to function, to control conflict, and to defend himself against anxiety depended in part on his particular role in the family, and the complementarity of the husband and wife roles, so the disturbance in the family's psychosocial interplay had manifested itself in his individual disturbance. Obviously he had been a vulnerable personality, but for eight years of courtship and nine years of marriage Mrs. B had supported, if not supplied, his social vitality and had shored up his defenses.

The Family as a Social System

It is evident from the above that the caseworkers gained additional crucial insights into the character of this young father's disturbance when they gained an understanding of other family members, and when they viewed the family as a field of interaction both in the present and in the past. Parenthetically it is noteworthy how often the members of the extended family have played decisive roles in the nuclear family's history. It has been observed for some time how important a role is played in a marriage by the unresolved relationships of each partner with his own parents. Beyond this psychological fact, however, meaningful social interaction with close relatives is surprisingly common in even the most urban and so-called isolated nuclear family. Dr. Hope Leichter's studies at Jewish Family Service on kinship and social casework promise important findings in this area.

Caseworkers often respond to new ideas as if they were to serve as replacements for old and accustomed concepts. So it is with proposals that are made in relation to examining the family as a total system. When family diagnosis and treatment are suggested, some workers become defensive, as if focus on the family is meant to replace individual diagnosis and treatment, rather than being an additional orientation. Clinical concepts are still needed for the diagnosis and treatment of the individual when he is viewed as part of his family. The family focus establishes chiefly a larger context, a social framework within which to assess individual psychological factors. It provides an integrational rather than a conjunctive approach to the understanding of psychological and social factors. In the B case, physical and social facts represent one side of the coin; subjective psychological experiences of each young parent are the other. A further examination of the details of this case reveals that the total functioning of Mrs. B as wife and mother, both in her subjective experiences and in her social performance, is not adequately explained by reference to either her personality alone or to the social and cultural conditioning of family roles. Nor is it adequately explained through the separate analysis of the psychological and the social factors. A holistic approach is the only one that permits the worker to develop a truly adequate understanding of the family and its various members.

Social Role

If an understanding of the family as an interactional system is to be added to that of the individual personality, theory must be constructed that will permit us to link the two. It has been suggested that the concept of social role can serve as the central link.[22] Whether or not it is the central one, the concept of social and family roles is of considerable usefulness. As has been so frequently pointed out, the family is a constant in all societies and inseparable from human existence. LaBarre has noted that, "What is changing historically and culturally is merely the adventitious local traits of the basic family. . . ."[23] The family's omnipresence and permanence are a result of its being the only institution that performs certain biological and social functions for the very continuance of human existence. In order for the family to fulfil its functions, the individuals within it occupy certain statuses and have certain tasks and roles to perform. The life of the family is, in part, a composite of the complex role processes of the individuals within it. Each individual is integrated within the family social system through the process of adaptation to family roles, or as Merton more aptly puts it, role sets.[24] The process of adaptation to roles is a biologic, psychic, interpersonal, and cultural process.

There has persisted in social work a tendency to view role adaptation as a non-psychological process and to view roles as merely socially and culturally determined models. This tendency

[22] Werner W. Boehm, *op. cit.*
[23] Weston LaBarre, "Appraising Today's Pressures on Family Living," *Social Casework,* Vol. XXXII, No. 2 (1951), p. 55.
[24] Robert K. Merton, "The Role Set: Problems in Sociological Theory," *British Journal of Sociology,* Vol VIII, No 2 (1957), pp. 106–120.

has probably derived from the fact that sociology is the source of role theory. Caseworkers have feared that an orientation toward family role processes courts the danger of neglecting the whole person. Frances Scherz has stated:

> Problems of interaction and communication in a family are not necessarily related to problems in social role functioning. . . . Whether treatment efforts . . . are directed primarily toward the stabilization or modification of social roles, or toward the support or modification of individual habitual modes of adaptation—including the use of defenses that militate against constructive functioning—seems to me to depend on an assessment that includes role performance as only one specific in the broad array of diagnostic and treatment determinants [25]

Inherent in this quotation, as in the positions taken by others, is a depersonalization of role processes and a conceptualization of family roles as *things* instead of processes. A mother does not perform the role of mother apart from her patterned way of controlling inner conflict, alleviating anxiety, and adapting to change. The way in which she mothers her child, how her mothering behavior interacts with her marital behavior, and her subjective experiences as a mother are all expressions of her total self.

It is imperative to conceptualize the integration of the psychological and the social, especially in family roles and role systems. Ego adaptive patterns are actually equivalent to—rather than identical with—how the individual adapts to roles, and how his roles and role interaction influence him. Separating the integration of roles and role interaction from the individual's ego adaptation is atomistic rather than integrational. Contributing further confusion to the problem is what is intended by the use of the term "social." This term certainly refers to institutions and artifacts, but I have used it here in its quintessential meaning of "interpersonal." With some modifications Mary Richmond's statement of over forty years ago still is relevant:

> It is true that the word *social* has many meanings. As it has been adapted in usage . . . it has a meaning at once more inclusive and more exclusive than some who glibly use the word seem to realize. The criterion of the social,

[25] Frances H Scherz, "Implications of the Curriculum Study for Staff Development," *Social Casework*, Vol. XL, No. 8 (1959), p. 439.

its indispensable element always, is the influence of mind upon mind. This influence may be exercised in a small group, such as the family, the kindred, or the other personal contacts of a given subject . . .[26]

Thus, from this broad definition of "social," we can develop the more specific concepts, such as family homeostasis, role adaptation, and so on, in the hope that we may bring to realization a workable family theory.

[26] Mary E. Richmond, *Proceedings of the National Conference of Social Work, 1917*, National Conference of Social Work, Chicago, 1918, p. 112.

A Review of Psychiatric Developments in Family Diagnosis and Family Therapy

Don D. Jackson and Virginia Satir

WE ARE PRESENTING our brief observations on the history of family diagnosis and therapy, we trust, more in the spirit of Toynbee than in the style of the *Encyclopaedia Brittanica*

We must begin by defining what we are including under the rubric "family diagnosis and therapy" because the designation of "family" as a treatment unit, in contrast to a uniform understanding of the individual as the treatment unit, means different things to different people. A family approach, we believe, requires an orientation stressing sociocultural forces and explicitly acknowledging more diagnostic and prognostic implications of the "here and now" situation than might be subscribed to by clinical therapists generally.

Technically, using the family as a treatment unit has been interpreted differently by different clinicians. The different approaches seem to fall into the following general categories:

1. The members of a biological or nuclear family are treated conjointly, which means that all family members are seen together at the same time by the same therapist. The members of the family include parents, children, other significant relatives such as grandparents and aunts or uncles, and other significant non-relative people, with the selection dependent on relationships and not necessarily on blood ties. This is our approach at the Mental Research Institute.

2. The members of a family are seen conjointly for diagnostic purposes, and family members are then assigned on an individual basis to different therapists who will work collaboratively. An-

other variation is to select one member for individual psycho-therapy after a family diagnosis has been made. It is our impres-sion that this latter practice is generally used when geographical circumstances, such as the patient's being in a hospital some dis-tance from his home, necessitate it.

3. Family members are seen individually from the outset by a single therapist who then pieces together the picture of family interaction and continues to treat the family members individually. Family members may also be seen individually from the outset, each by a different therapist. The therapists then sit down together to pool their findings to try to arrive at a picture of family interaction —perhaps in much the same spirit as the family itself might do— with subsequent individual treatment. The family interaction is observed primarily at the level of collaboration.

All the above approaches are predicated on the necessity for viewing the symptoms of the identified patient or patients within the total family interaction, with the explicit theoretical belief that there is a relationship between the symptom of the identified patient and the total family interaction. The extent to which the therapist "believes" in family therapy will determine his empha-sis on techniques that convey this orientation to the patient.

4. In another form of working with the family, the identified patient is seen in individual psychotherapy and family members are seen occasionally to determine how best to elicit their aid, or simply to urge them not to interfere with the patient's progress. We feel the utility of this method is limited. It is based on the theoretical concept that the patient alone is a sick unit, and that the other family members are well and capable of change in the interest of the patient. This approach emphasizes the existence of two units within the family—the identified patient as the sick unit and the other family members as the well unit.

It seems to us that, for clarity's sake, "family" should refer to parents and children (or other persons who are a part of the immediate social family), and the terms "diagnosis" and "therapy," and "concurrent," "conjoint," or "collaborative" should be em-ployed to designate the exact nature of the technique being used.

A search of the *Cumulus Medicus* for the past thirty years for papers in which the noun "family" appears, reveals that this designation relates to methods of study or treatment that can be considered "family oriented." We believe the terms "family diagnosis" and "therapy" should be restricted to those systems of study where the therapist's impression of state X in subject A carries probability statements about subject B; if B is in the same nuclear family and at a different level, A's inferences about B change A's probable state (behavior, motivation, and so on) from X to X_1, X_2, and so on. In individual therapy, the focus tends to be on how A feels about B or about himself, without shifting levels.

One final point in connection with terminology. Although it is possible to label what is meant by "the family," and to label the approaches used to the family as a unit, the language used in theoretical descriptions about family interaction reveals the need to find new and more appropriate terminology that may correctly define the concepts. Writers attempting to explain concepts of family interaction seem to be struggling to apply to family interaction terminology that is useful in describing individual therapy, with resulting unclear conclusions. At the present time, if we were able to find a common denominator in all the literature about description and analysis of family interaction, we would have a greater pool of common observations and probably greater agreement about their significance.

Some Influential Factors

The following general factors seem to us crucial in contributing to the development of family-oriented rather than individually-oriented psychological observation and treatment.

1. Psychiatry, since the late 19th century, has been gradually losing its fraternal position to medicine and is becoming instead a cousin who, though a blood relative, springs from a different family. Psychology, sociology, and anthropology are increasingly influencing the kind of psychological data obtained and the nature of the interpretation given these data. For example, it has been recently reported that eldest sons of Indian families living in Singapore are many times more vulnerable to a schizophrenic

psychosis than any other member of the Indian family or any of the members of the Chinese or Malayan families who constitute the other two main ethnic groups.[27] * Such a finding surely must eventually influence the diagnostic and therapeutic approach to the patient who is an Indian eldest son. Thus, in this simple example, we see how anthropology and sociology may make direct contributions to the etiology of emotional illness and consequently influence psychiatric practice.

2. The child guidance movement, which was initially developed through efforts of the juvenile court to treat delinquent children specifically, rather naturally expanded to look for and include expeditious and economical means to diagnose and treat neurotic and psychotic children. Experience, especially on the part of social workers, has led to the conclusion that treating the child is not enough and, more recently, that treating the child and the mother may not be enough. In 1942, Mildred Burgum published a paper [9] in which she demonstrated by statistics from a child guidance clinic that the father's role was ignored in the early approach to the family and that this fact might account for a high drop-out rate. Such findings have gradually become incorporated in child guidance practices. If the clinic is to keep the father involved, however, it means further manpower problems for the clinic and thus a push in the direction of family therapy. Our own group has discovered that the child who is labeled by the family as the patient is not necessarily the "sickest" in the family. Such datum casts doubt on the wisdom of seeing only the identified patient and the mother. A family approach thus comes to offer increased data that were not always available under the older methods, as well as possibilities for increased economy and research.

3. The psychoanalytic movement, which has been so largely responsible for loosening the ties between classical medicine and psychiatry, has been a prime influence in family diagnosis. Flügel, in *The Psycho-Analytic Study of the Family*, the first book of its kind, states, "It is probable that the chief practical gain that may result from the study of the psychology of the family will ensue more or less directly from the mere increase in understanding the nature

* In this article the reference numbers refer to the bibliography at the end of the article.

of, and interactions between, the mental processes that are involved in family relationships." [11]

a. Although psychoanalysis is a system that focuses on the individual, reference to the family has been appearing since Freud's case of little Hans. The classical Oedipus situation, originally an intrapsychic construct, has become increasingly interpersonal especially as the mother's pregenital influence has come to be recogmized. The sociologist, Parsons, and others have expanded Freud's original notion into the broader framework of anthropology and sociology. The emphasis on ego psychology since the 1920's and the writings of the so-called neo-Freudian psychoanalysts have become increasingly interactive or transactional and thus have focused on the patient's significance to others, usually his family. Even the emphasis on intrapsychic objects by Klein, Fairbairn, Windicott, and others stirs a curiosity to discover these objects in the real world.

b. Freud's extreme position in relation to the relatives of the patient has led to a re-examination of his position and, on the part of some analysts, to a search for more workable arrangements Freud issued an urgent warning against any attempt to engage the confidence or support of parents or relatives, confessing that he had little faith in any individual treatment of them. It was inevitable that individuals like Mittelman and Oberndorf would be challenged to test these dicta and thus lead to further developments toward a family concept.

c. Another influence toward family studies, which has indirectly stemmed from the psychoanalytic movement, has to do with the disappointment in the results of this expensive and time-consuming technique and the possible relation of results to a change in the type of clinical material with which psychoanalysts deal. The shift in emphasis from symptom neuroses to character, marital, and child guidance problems has resulted in a broadening of analytic techniques with an emphasis on parameters and on psychoanalytically oriented psychotherapy.

d. Child analysis failed to fulfil its initial promises as analysts discovered that even five one-hour sessions a week could not keep up, in most cases, with the influences of the remaining 163 hours at home. The number of child analysts who have stuck to their last is surprisingly small, and this fact must have had some influence in giving tacit approval for others to seek new techniques in treating children.

Thus, psychoanalysis has acted both in a positive and in a negative sense to expedite the family movement and it is obvious that many of the authorities on family diagnosis and therapy are psychoanalytically trained. This latter factor has contributed to a complication of which we shall speak later—the current lack of a language for family diagnosis and therapy.

4 Gradually an awareness has been developing of the existence of health within the same framework in which pathology exists, which has led to a beginning re-evaluation of the prognosis of emotional illness. The concept of "adaptation" has helped focus on the "why" of the illness rather than on fixed psychopathological symptoms. Jahoda's recent book on mental health and mental illness [18] introduces dimensions of health and emphasizes the needs to see the "sick person" or "sick family" in dimensions of health as well as illness. A diagnosis of a sick person described entirely in terms of pathology often presents a dreary, hopeless picture. None but the most brave, foolish, or dedicated would attempt the apparently hopeless. However, a visit to the home, a sesssion with the whole family, can reveal to the therapist unsuspected pockets of ability of family members to relate, to share a joke, or even to be a little kind to each other.

5. Another important factor in the development of a family approach has emerged from the psychotherapy of schizophrenia which blossomed in the thirties and underwent an increased growth rate during the forties. Federn and others thought that the schizophrenic's irrepressible id created an atmophere in which the therapist needed to focus on current situations and actual experience. Sullivan, from a somewhat different point of view, advised the same procedure and cautioned that reality factors existed as a kernel in all the patient's distorted productions. These points of view brought the therapist more in contact with the patient's real experience within his family, and this practice was strengthened by the eloquent writings of Fromm-Reichmann. In addition, the hospital management of schizophrenics involved visits from relatives and led to a suspicion that these relatives were difficult people

to handle. It is interesting that a recent report by G. W. Brown of the Maudsley Hospital confirms the validity of this early suspicion.[8] He demonstrated that the success or failure of chronic schizophrenic patients after leaving the hospital depended on whether they returned to their parents or spouse, or were able to live alone in a lodging or with siblings. The highest failure was in those returning to their parents and in those returning to a spouse and *was not related to their diagnosis or to their prognosis on admission.* On the other hand, if a married patient was able to return to his spouse and remain outside the hospital over three months, he achieved a higher level of social adjustment than any of the other schizophrenics studied. Other recent studies have revealed that the single most significant correlate with the patient's length of stay in the hospital was the number of visits he received during his first two months of hospitalization.[10, 37] In the face of such discoveries, it becomes increasingly difficult for the therapist of the schizophrenic to remain purely patient-oriented.

6. A final factor is an augmentation of point 1, concerning the growth of anthropology, psychology, and sociology and their increasing clinical orientation. A psychiatrist interested in the family would not think of ignoring the work of Parsons and Bales,[28] any more than he would overlook Ackerman's recent book.[1] Two of the most promising avenues of exploration of family interaction lie in the field of social psychology and its study of small groups and in the field of communication and information theory, largely peopled by experimental and clinical psychologists.

The factors that we have mentioned are not mutually exclusive and interdigitate in a way that makes it difficult to tease them apart. For example, the child mental health program was largely conducted in clinics where non-psychiatrists did the bulk of the work and where finances were of great moment. In the search for efficacious brief methods it was a recognized fact that a social worker could more properly interview parents than could a psychoanalyst since the latter would be uncomfortable in crossing tradition-bound lines that dedicated him to a single patient. On the other hand, the fact that a good deal of family work has evolved from interest in schizophrenia is due to slightly different combinations of circumstances. Schizophrenia, an increasingly important illness with no predictable means of cure, was psychologically everyone's baby but no one's baby, and therefore analysts, psychiatrists, and social scientists were free to contribute to and experiment in its treatment.

Whatever the various factors contributing to the evolution of family diagnosis and therapy, one thread runs rather clearly through the history of modern psychoanalytically-oriented psychiatry. This is the gradual development of concepts from a monadic viewpoint to dyadic and currently, triadic or larger. Even though Flügel saw the need of studying family members, he used his study of individual family members and of family systems in order to increase the knowledge of the individual. His approach, therefore, is essentially monadic. We have not come a great distance from his position, as witness the words of Spiegel and Bell:

Practice may or may not follow theory faithfully. The dynamic theories of psychopathology and the findings derived through their use have been largely individual-centered. However, these theories have been constructed in such a way that the individual is conceived as a self-contained system becoming relatively closed early in life. Even the social and cultural variance of these theories share this assumption. *We do not find evidence that treatment procedures vary significantly* from what one would expect on the basis of theory. In the context of the habitual lip-service paid to the family as a whole, isolated groups or individuals have attempted to maintain a focus on a family unit in diagnostic formulations and treatment procedures but attempts to bring the family to the forefront have not been established.[39]

The one portion of this statement we wish to disagree with is the authors' claim that there are no treatment procedures that vary significantly. It seems to us that Nathan Ackerman's treatment of a family at the Family Mental Health Clinic and our own approach at the Mental Research Institute are significantly different from any recognized method of individual therapy. It is possible that some therapists would be shocked at what goes on in family therapy because the approach is so much a transactional one rather than a careful hovering attention to the individual's apparent thoughts and feelings.

The literature reveals relatively little that could be described as organized formulations that would set the theoretical base of those who diagnose and treat emotional illness of a labeled patient as a part of sick family interaction, apart from the theory underlying the treatment of an individual. The reason may be that concepts surrounding individual diagnoses and treatment are pretty universally accepted and form the primary content of respectable professional training. Much of the writing deals with the family in relation to schizophrenia, a disorder that is set apart from neuroses and has not had an important part in psychoanalytic theory. Any resemblance between interaction in families where schizophrenia exists and interaction in families where other forms of emotional illness exist is difficult for some individuals to accept. In the same vein, these same individuals make a sharp distinction between the techniques of treating schizophrenic patients and non-psychotic patients.

Events Leading to Acceptance of Conjoint Treatment

After some soul-searching and much library searching we would like to present some of the events that we believe have played an important part in the relatively new idea of conjoint family diagnosis and therapy. We use schizophrenia as a model for simplicity's sake and because of our greater familiarity with this subject.

The following events are some of the high spots in the approach to conjoint work with the families of schizophrenics—a type of treatment that is apparently less than ten years of age.

1911: Freud wrote his famous Schreber case.[18] The dynamics of paranoia were discussed and were seen to have defensive aspects and underlying dynamics which made schizophrenia more than a cerebral defect. Incidentally, in the description of this case are allusions to "wife" and "mother" which are of interest to students of schizophrenia.

1916: Rudin's monograph on the genetics of schizophrenia appeared.[84] Patients' families were interviewed and a connection was made between their difficulties and the patients'. During the twenties and thirties some of Rudin's students published further studies of the families of schizophrenic index cases. Especially important were those studies in which the children of schizophrenic parents were examined and found to evince many mental disorders including neuroses and manic-depressive disorder. Although the approach was biological, the schizophrenic and his family were

37

nevertheless brought together for study and the lack of nice Mendelian findings raised the question of social forces.

1920: Moreno and others began group psychotherapy with hospitalized patients.[26] The whole group therapy movement has had a definite, if not obvious, effect on family theory and therapy, since it pointed up the value of analyzing interaction as it occurred between individuals. Through witnessing interaction, the group therapist was able to improve his diagnosis. Identifying interaction and interpreting this interaction in terms of motivation were means by which psychological growth was enhanced.

1927: Sullivan reported on his spectacular work with schizophrenics at the Sheppard and Enoch Pratt Hospital,[41] where the transactions that went on between the hospital personnel and the patients were seen to lead to behavioral changes when the response on the part of the staff member was changed so that it did not meet the patient's usual expectations as he had come to experience this in his own family. Sullivan saw that, in the patient's mind, the staff was an extension of his family and that he responded and dealt with them in the same way. Thus, Sullivan emphasized the importance of the hospital family, that is the physician, nurses, and aides, in contributing to the patient's recovery.

1934: Kasinin and his colleagues described the parent-child relationship of some schizophrenics and implied that this relationship was an important and specific etiological factor.[20] Later Kasinin described a pair of identical twins discordant for schizophrenia and described differences in their relationship vis-à-vis the family.

1934: Hallowell published an article on culture and mental disorder,[14] one of the early attempts to demonstrate the importance of social factors in psychoses.

1938· Ackerman wrote on "The Unity of the Family," [2] conceptualizing a clinical purpose in viewing the family as an entity when dealing with individual disturbance.

1939: Beaglehole published a ten-year study of schizophrenia in New Zealand [5] comparing the incidence in the white and native Maori populations. The difference was great enough to invite the citing of family and culture as possible causative factors.

38

1939: Pollock and others published *Heredity and Environmental Factors in the Causation of Manic-Depressive Psychoses and Dementia Praecox.*[31] Among other things, this volume indicated that schizophrenic patients might have a special position in the family, for example, being the more financially dependent.

1939: Abram Kardiner's book, *The Individual and His Family,* appeared.[19]

1943: Sherman and Kraines published an article entitled "Environmental and Personality Factors in Psychoses." [36]

1944: L. S. Penrose described mental illness in husband and wife as a contribution to the study of associative mating, where essentially it was postulated that mate selection might be a means of groping for health.[29]

1945: Richardson brought forth his book, *Patients Have Families.*[33] This was in part an attempt to formulate some family disgnoses rather than treating the individual vis-à-vis his family group.

1950: Reichard and Tillman published an article entitled "Patterns of Parent-Child Relationships in Schizophrenia." [32]

1950: Ackerman and Sobel wrote "Family Diagnosis: An Approach to the Pre-School Child," [3] which inverted the typical child guidance approach and highlighted the understanding of family processes as a means of understanding the young child.

1951: Ruesch and Bateson published their famous book, *Communication, the Social Matrix of Psychiatry.*[35] Many of their contributions foreshadowed the current interest in communication, information theory, and feedback mechanisms.

1954: Stanton and Schwartz published *The Mental Hospital.*[40] Among other important contributions was their discovery that acute upsets in schizophrenic patients' therapy coincided with a covert disagreement between the administrator and the therapist. A similar phenomenon in the family context was discussed recently in a paper by Weakland and Jackson.[48]

1954: Wahl described antecedent factors in the histories of 392 schizophrenics.[42] The importance of psychological and family events stood out clearly in this group of young males hospitalized while in the military service.

1954: John Spiegel published a paper, "New Perspectives in the Study of the Family." [38] A later report of the Committee on the Family of the Group for the Advancement of Psychiatry, prepared by Kluckhohn and Spiegel,[21] has become a classic in this field.

1954: Jackson presented a paper to the American Psychiatric Association entitled "The Question of Family Homeostasis," [17] in which he described some psychological upsets occurring in family members in relation to improvement on the part of the identified patient. Parental interaction patterns were tentatively related to specific symptoms in the patient and the concept "schizophrenogenic mother" was rejected as being incomplete and misleading.

1956: Bateson and others presented some ideas on a communication theory of schizophrenia which were based, in part, on conjoint therapy with schizophrenic patients and their families.[4]

1957: Bowen presented a paper at the American Orthopsychiatric Association entitled "Study and Treatment of Five Hospitalized Family Groups Each with a Psychotic Member." [7] His findings, based on the most intensive family study ever undertaken, supported the findings of Lidz and others who had observed the fluctuating nature of symptoms from one family member to another as changes within the family interaction were taking place. Further, there was the observation that the nature and kind of symptom bore a strong resemblance to the content and nature of the total family interaction.

1957: Midelfort published *The Family and Psychotherapy*.[25] Working in a small Wisconsin community, he capitalized on the hospital's traditional use of relatives to assist in the care of the patients, by involving families of schizophrenics and depressed patients in brief therapy.

1957: Lidz and his co-workers published "The Intra-familial Environment of the Schizophrenic Patient." [24] They have subsequently published a number of outstanding papers in this area.

40

1958: Wynne and others described "Pseudo-Mutuality in the Family Relationships of Schizophrenics" [45] in which they stressed the discrepancy between a superficial and a deeper look at these families.

The way in which ideas about family therapy and diagnosis have come about is clearly evolutionary rather than revolutionary. The impetus was provided by the continuing search for further knowledge about the causes of mental and emotional illness and a more effective means of treatment.

As one looks over the literature of the last fifty years, one notes the patchwork pattern, in a chronological sense, of reports of successful treatment results that came about through a new method of treatment or new knowledge about the causes of illness. When one assembles and analyzes these reports, the direction toward our present concepts about treating illness as an integral part of the total family interaction can be seen as slowly evolving and inevitable.

At the present time there is not yet a well-defined, total, conceptual framework for diagnosis and treatment of the family, but some isolated brave souls have provided us with important experiences and research findings which, if integrated, may well be the beginning of a validatable conceptual framework.

Special Contributions

Since 1958, the number of contributions that could be listed would more than equal the brief and incomplete list already given. From the above chronological list we have omitted several names only to offer them special mention. They are Eugen Bleuler, Adolph Meyer, and Manfred Bleuler. Among them, they have exerted tremendous influence in bridging the vast gulf in conceptualizing relative influences on human behavior from neurone to family. Bleuler devoted more of his famous book [6] to the so-called secondary symptoms of schizophrenia than to the primary ones, and laid the basis for psychological therapy in this disorder, particularly by his humanitarian approach and his observations on the patients' response to human contact. Adolph Meyer, originally

41

a neuropathologist, stressed the individual's experiences, present and past, and helped bring schizophrenia out from under the microscope. The life history form that Meyer evolved must have brought parental characteristics to the attention of his students even though the parents were not present in the flesh. Many American psychiatrists have stressed their debt to Meyer, including Sullivan and two of his students, Leo Kanner and Theodore Lidz, and have contributed much to our understanding of family interaction in the schizophrenic disorders. Finally, to Manfred Bleuler goes the credit for synthesizing the methods of population genetics, and he and Boök have removed the focus of the schizophrenic genetic study from the index case to the epidemiology of local populations. Bleuler's interest is indicated by the fact that when one of his associates discovered eight of the families of fifty schizophrenic index cases were reported in the hospital chart as normal, he went to visit them in their homes and made his own observations. He was, needless to say, disillusioned about the good impression they had made at the hospital.

The early association of the schizophrenic family, via the suggestion of poor protoplasm, with mental illness, mental deficiency, criminality, epilepsy, and tuberculosis has undergone sweeping changes, and yet these very studies unwittingly helped us focus on the "family" as an object of study. As evidence for the hereditary or infectious etiology of mental and social disorders waned, it was a natural step to ask, "All right, but why do they appear to be familial?" Perhaps the familial incidence of pellagra and the subsequent discovery of its relation to family eating habits played a part in this shift of emphasis.

It is obvious then that the family approach owes much to many and that these contributors have been from both the biological and the psychological sides of the fence. We realize that it is not considered good form to dichotomize; yet such dichotomy does very strongly exist in our science Using the family as a treatment unit seems to us to be a recognition that the patient does not get sick alone, nor does he get well alone. Furthermore, it is consistent with a common observation: that people direct love, hate, fear, and destructiveness toward someone, which implies interaction; done by oneself, such action does not count for much.

42

Conjoint family therapy validates the widely accepted personality theory that the learning about handling love, hate, anger, and fear takes place in the nuclear family. In our opinion this learning then becomes the basis upon which any family interaction is shaped. By the nature of things, it influences the development of individual self-esteem and consequently the individual's behavior.

Predictions and Portents

Since no red-blooded historian these days is content merely to report, we shall take the liberty of naming current trends and possible future trends that we feel will be important in shaping the development and outcome of family diagnosis and therapy. These trends will be listed under certain topics for the sake of convenience.

1. Psychoanalysis

We feel that just as events point to increasing union between psychiatry, the family, and social science, there will be no such union in the main current of psychoanalysis for some time to come. Although there is a small group of psychoanalysts who are interested in participating in family studies and research, there is a much larger group who do not consider this work immediately relevant to their own interests, and even a rather hard-bitten group who feel that current family approaches are superficial and tangential and can in no way be compared scientifically with the depth analysis of psychoanalytic therapy. There is also a group of well meaning psychoanalysts who are attempting to correlate and collate family data with their own observations as individuals, but who unwittingly do the family movement a disservice. This is because some of them feel that knowledge about family individuals is old stuff and is now merely being refurbished. Their descriptions of family work are largely couched in the monadic framework of psychoanalytic terminology and are still essentially individual. They have not yet become convinced that the parts are greater than the whole; their main tenet is that the treatment of a family is theoretically impractical because of the difficulty the therapist has in handling more than one transference at the same time. This latter observation is part of the reason why family diagnosis and therapy needs a new terminology since the concept of transference

43

cannot be carried over in its entirety from monadic encounters on the couch to experiences a single therapist has with multiple family members.

We feel that the concept of family diagnosis and therapy owes much of its current position to psychoanalysis. We predict that there will be an increasing divergence between the two groups. The divergence is due partly to the inapplicability of psychoanalytic terminology to family work, and partly to the fact that the majority of analysts will probably remain interested in their own line of endeavor and find the shift to a family orientation rather difficult to make. This situation has not been unknown to science previously. Witness the findings in electromagnetics of Clark and Maxwell, and the change in concepts following Einstein's contributions. The observations of the electromagnetic theorists were not rejected because a broader conceptualization made its appearance. The current scene reveals evidence of friction and we hope the struggle will not produce a generation of fence-sitters who are waiting to see how the whole business comes out, but will instead serve to stimulate all clinicians to look at all new data rationally and objectively.

2. The Social Sciences

In contrast to its relationship with psychoanalysis, the future of the diagnosis and therapy of the family through its linkage with the social sciences appears very promising. Several recent and current efforts point up possible avenues for exploration.

a. The family is seen as the unit of health, both physical and psychological, a concept crystallized by the publication of Richardson's book, *Patients Have Families*.[33] We all have experienced or have been aware of episodic outbreaks of various illnesses in families. Even such an obvious factor as contagion does not always explain these outbreaks and many times there appear to be inexplicable combinations of infections, psychosomatic disorders, and "accidents." Just as we know little about the siblings of the identified patient, we know next to nothing about family disease patterns.

b. Foote and Cottrell in *Identity and Interpersonal Competence*,[12] and Parson and Bales in their volume on family interaction [28] have pioneered efforts to devise operational definitions and measurements describing families.

44

c. Spiegel and Kluckhohn have focused on family cultural patterns and taught us not to mix our observations indiscriminately. It appears that the family researcher has to be pro-segregation or his generalizations will not hold up.

d. Similarly in the socioeconomic arena, Kohn and Clausen,[22] Hollingshead and Redlich,[16] and others have indicated important differences in families as far as their socioeconomic level and their beliefs, values, and child-rearing practices are concerned. Kohn has found in his Washington studies that the mother is the accepted head of the household in most of his lower-class material.* What adjustments, then, must one make in using the term "Oedipus complex" if he would generalize from lower- to middle-class families?

e. Pollak, in his work at the Jewish Board of Guardians, has demonstrated how invaluable the efforts of a sociologist may be in shaping psychopathological concepts.[30] His approach escapes from the closed system of psychiatric nosology and his concepts lend themselves to further expansion by other workers.

f. Westley and Epstein at McGill University are demonstrating the importance of choosing a healthy index case rather than the traditional sick one.[44] If their conclusions are verified—for example, that some of their healthy subjects come from homes wherein the parents maintain an atrocious sex life—then some of the basic concepts we have borrowed from psychoanalysis and indiscriminately used in studying the family need careful scrutiny.

g. Finally, I want to mention one of the outstanding and certainly most indefatigable workers in the family area, Reuben Hill.[15] He and his associates at the University of Minnesota are assaying the entire literature of marriage and the family with the idea of organizing concepts, pointing up promising leads, and outlining areas of conflicting data.

Conclusion

None of us knows what system or systems will be worked out in the area of family diagnosis and therapy, but without doubt they will differ greatly from anything that currently appears in psychiatric textbooks. The possibilities are legion, but the current

* Melvin L. Kohn, personal communication.

emphasis on data-processing via machines will probably influence the development of family description.

The importance of social sciences in this area probably means a greater focus on systems of health, rather than disease, which has been the traditional occupation of psychiatrists. Current promising concepts include family homeostasis, coalitions within the family and their stability, role-playing, acquisition of family models, three-generation theory, the theoretical applications of the game theory, decision-making, recognition of resemblance, and so on.

In our own work at the Mental Research Institute, we have been tremendously impressed with such a simple matter as the difference in goal-directedness of healthy versus psychologically sick families. During a structured interview, the family is asked to plan something together—a trip, a vacation, an acquisition, anything. The healthier family seems to operate on the premise that the good of the individual rests in the greatest good for all. Even lively sparks of sibling rivalry fail to get the family machinery off its course; the operation seems unequivocally focused on the goal, rather than on the relationships between the family members who are trying to achieve that goal. The sicker families have difficulty even in fantasying that they might plan something as a group; should they attempt a plan, one member is apt to comment at a meta level about another's suggestion. That is, it becomes not a question of whether A prefers the beach. There is great harkening back to the past and even jumping to the future with the implication that it doesn't make any difference since it will not work out anyhow. Such processes as co-operation, collaboration, and compromise can be studied microscopically in small sections of recorded interviews and related to the enormous literature in social psychology on the nature of small group process. Family movies help us discover learned mannerisms, disqualifications, via nonverbal behavior, and so on.

Another way of studying family interaction is to adumbrate a set of explicit and implicit rules under which the family appears to be operating, which can be observed clinically in terms of what family members may or may not overtly expect of each other. If this notion has any value, we eventually hope to find differences in

46

rules, and rules about rules, in psychologically healthy versus psychologically ill families. For example, it is our impression that the family of the chronic schizophrenic is guided by a rigid set of rules which are largely covert. These families do not like to think of themselves as being rigid and they do not explicitly acknowledge what the rules are. When a rule is made more explicit, it automatically is called into question and this produces family anxiety. Rules may be called into question if they are stated too overtly. A may challenge a particular rule and B will then point out how this particular rule does not fit in this particular instance. Rules may be called into question if a member threatens withdrawal from the group. It may be one of the covert rules not to acknowledge the possibility of independence. Withdrawal may be interpreted as rebellion against certain rules. The particular rule that A is alleged to be rebelling against may be revealed by the kind of implication the other family members attribute to his reason for withdrawal. Rules are called into question if they are exposed to an outsider's opinion; for example, the opinion of the therapist. This may mean some tricky foot work for the therapist if he is to keep the show on the road.

On the other hand, if rules are too closely followed, then a skew will result because the enforcement of each rule becomes a caricature of previous rules and a model for future ones. This was observed during the 1930's by Lasswell in his work with large companies.[23] He noted that if the boss was a short man with a bow tie and a cigar, the assistant boss would be even shorter with an even bigger cigar. Similarly, the schizophrenic patient is apt to caricature the rules in his family. It is this behavior that becomes labeled as "sick" by the family and may provoke both laughter and anger on their part. Generally, the sick family will attribute the greatest evil possible to the breaking of a rule, but at the same time they may excuse it. This contradictory behavior is not unknown in government. If a citizen complains, he may be labeled as unpatriotic and a scoundrel; if he does not complain he may suffer from gross inequities. Rationalizations are invaluable in handling such situations whether they are claims that the opposition is trying to cause trouble or, as in a family, the parents claim that the school system is outmoded and additionally that their child happened to get the worst teacher in school. All these maneuvers result in denying and obscuring the facts. A family governed by a rigid set of covert rules finds itself unable to deal with the vicissitudes of life, whether pleasurable or painful, and yet the family pact to hold to the rules may give to outsiders the illusion of strength. The inadequacy of the rules is shown by their not being discussed or debated and by the family's rationalizing each unfortunate happening as a separate chance matter. This concept of rules can be very directly translated into the therapeutic effort. For example, one family had a rule that the mother treasured loyalty above all else and had a right to feel hurt if a family member were critical of her, especially if this should happen within earshot of an outsider. A therapist was able to convince the husband that *true* loyalty demanded that he be able to be critical of his wife (if only via thought), since true loyalty consists in relating to the total person including both his assets and liabilities To relate only to the assumed assets would be merely blind following.

When communication within the family is studied, data about health and pathology become available. The social scientist, lacking the bias toward disease that is part of medical training, is in a better position than the psychiatrist to do research in this area.

Summary

In general, it is our impression that family diagnosis and therapy have come a long way from the classic monadic descriptions of early psychoanalysis. The trend, influenced by many contributions from many fields, has been toward a horizontal and a vertical expansion. Horizontally, more members have been included, more cultures and more socioeconomic data. Vertically, levels of interaction, communication, and information have been taken into consideration to replace a simple stimulus-response description, or more colloquially, a "who did *what* to whom" orientation.

Currently, the crying need seems to be for a useful language to describe multilevel interaction. Even a single message is multileveled, and the response is multileveled and related in a complex way to the first message. The context adds at least another level.

With regard to therapy specifically, we feel that all psychotherapies are related to change and growth and that conjoint family therapy offers one of the most impressive laboratories for studying growth and change available to the researcher. In only the last few years, many aspects of the individual's emotional growth or lack of it that would previously have been labeled "constitutional" have been interpreted as part of the matrix of family interaction.

Bibliography

1. Nathan W Ackerman, *The Psychodynamics of Family Life*, Basic Books, New York, 1958.

2 ——————, "The Unity of the Family," *Archives of Pediatrics*, Vol. LV, No. 1 (1938), pp 51–62

8 —————— and Raymond Sobel, "Family Diagnosis. An Approach to the Pre-School Child," *American Journal of Orthopsychiatry*, Vol. XX, No. 4 (1950), pp. 744–753

4. Gregory Bateson, Don D. Jackson, Jay Haley, and John H. Weakland, "Toward a Theory of Schizophrenia," *Behavioral Science*, Vol 1, No. 4 (1956), pp 251–264.

5. Ernest Beaglehole, *Social Change in the South Pacific*, Macmillan Co, New York, 1958.

6. Eugen Bleuler, *Dementia Praecox, or the Group of Schizophrenias*, Interternational Universities Press, New York, 1952.

7. Murray Bowen, Robert H. Dysinger, Warren M. Brodey, and Betty Basamania, "Study and Treatment of Five Hospitalized Family Groups Each with a Psychotic Member," read at the Annual Meeting of the American Orthopsychiatric Association, Chicago, Ill., March 8, 1957.

8. George W. Brown, "Experiences of Discharged Chronic Schizophrenic Patients in Various Types of Living Group," *Milbank Memorial Fund Quarterly*, Vol XXXVII, No 2 (1959), pp. 105–131.

9 Mildred Burgum, "The Father Gets Worse: A Child Guidance Problem," *American Journal of Orthopsychiatry*, Vol. XII, No 3 (1942), pp. 474–485.

10. G. Morris Carstairs, and G W. Brown, (Maudsley Hospital,, London, England), "A Census of Psychiatric Cases in Two Contrasting Communities," *Journal of Mental Science*, Vol. CIV, No. 434 (1958), pp. 72–81.

11. J. C. Flügel, *The Psycho-Analytic Study of the Family*, Hogarth Press, London, 1921, p. 217.

12. Nelson Foote and Leonard S. Cottrell, Jr., *Identity and Interpersonal Competence*, University of Chicago Press, Chicago, 1955.

13. Sigmund Freud, "Psycho-Analytic Notes upon an Autobiographical Account of a Case of Paranoia," *Vol. III. Collected Papers*, Basic Books, New York, 1959, pp. 387–416.

14. A. Irving Hallowell, "Culture and Mental Disorder," *Journal of Abnormal and Social Psychiatry*, Vol. XXIX, No. 1 (1934), pp 1–9.

15. Reuben Hill, "A Critique of Contemporary Marriage and Family Research," *Social Forces*, Vol. XXXIII, No. 3 (1955), pp. 268–277.

16 August B. Hollingshead and Frederick C. Redlich, *Social Class and Mental Illness*, John Wiley and Sons, New York, 1958.

17. Don D. Jackson, "The Question of Family Homeostasis," *Psychiatric Quarterly Supplement*, Vol. XXXI, No. 1 (1957), pp. 79–90.

18. Marie Jahoda, *Current Concepts of Positive Mental Health*, Basic Books, New York, 1958

19. Abram Kardiner, *The Individual and His Family*, Columbia University Press, New York, 1939.

20. Jacob Kasanin, Elizabeth Knight, and Priscilla Sage, "The Parent-Child Relationship in Schizophrenia," *Journal of Nervous and Mental Disease*, Vol. LXXIX, No. 3 (1934), pp. 249–263.

21 Florence R. Kluckhohn and John P. Spiegel, "Integration and Conflict in Family Behavior," Report No. 27, Group for the Advancement of Psychiatry, Topeka, Kansas, 1954

22 Melvin L. Kohn and John A. Clausen, "Social Isolation and Schizophrenia," *American Sociological Review*, Vol. XX, No. 3 (1955), pp. 265–273.

23. Lasswell, Harold D., *The Psychopathology of Politics*, University of Chicago Press, Chicago, 1930.

24. Theodore Lidz, *et al.*, "The Intrafamilial Environment of the Schizophrenic Patient, I. The Father," *Psychiatry*, Vol. XX, No. 4 (1957), pp. 329–342

25. Christian F. Midelfort, *The Family in Psychotherapy*, McGraw-Hill, New York, 1957

26. Jacob L. Moreno, *The First Book on Group Psychotherapy*, 5th ed., Beacon House, New York, 1957.

27. H. B. M. Murphy, "Culture and Mental Disorder in Singapore," *Culture and Mental Health*, Marvin K. Opler (ed.), Macmillan Co., New York, 1959, pp. 291–316.

28. Talcott Parsons and Robert F Bales, *Family Socialization and Interaction Process*, Free Press, Glencoe, Ill , 1955

29. Lionel S Penrose, "Mental Illness in Husband and Wife: A Contribution to the Study of Associative Mating," *Psychiatric Quarterly Supplement*, Vol. XVIII, No. 2 (1944), pp. 161–166.

30. Otto Pollak, *Integrative Sociological and Psychoanalytic Concepts*, Russell Sage Foundation, New York, 1956.

31. Horatio M. Pollock *et al.*, *Heredity and Environmental Factors in the Causation of Manic-Depressive Psychoses and Dementia Praecox*, State Hospitals Press, Utica, New York, 1939

32. Suzanne Reichard and Carl Tillman, "Patterns of Parent-Child Relationships in Schizophrenia," *Psychiatry*, Vol. XIII, No. 2 (1950), pp. 247–257.

33. Henry B. Richardson, *Patients Have Families*, Commonwealth Fund, New York, 1945.

34. E. Rudin, "Vererbung und Enstehung geistiger Störungen, I. Zur Vererbung und Neuentstehung der Dementia Praecox," *Monographien aus dem Gesamt-Gebiete der Neurologie und Psychiatrie*, Vol. XII, Springer, Berlin, 1916.

35. Jurgen Ruesch and Gregory Bateson, *Communication, the Social Matrix of Psychiatry*, W. W. Norton, New York, 1951.

36. Irene C. Sherman and Samuel S Kraines, "Environmental and Personality Factors in Psychoses," *Journal of Nervous and Mental Disease*, Vol. XCVII, No 6 (1943), pp. 676–691.

37. Robert Sommer, "Visitors to Mental Hospials," *Mental Hygiene*, Vol. XL, No. 1 (1959), pp. 8–15.

38. John P Spiegel, "New Perspectives in the Study of the Family," *Marriage and Family Living*, Vol. XVI, No 1 (1954), pp. 4–12.

39. ————— and Norman W. Bell, "The Family of the Psychiatric Patient," *American Handbook of Psychiatry*, Vol. I, Basic Books, New York, 1959, p. 134

40. Alfred H. Stanton and Morris S. Schwartz, *The Mental Hospital*, Basic Books, New York, 1954.

41. Harry Stack Sullivan, "The Onset of Schizophrenia," *American Journal of Psychiatry*, Vol. VII, (1927), pp. 105–134.

42. Charles W. Wahl, "Some Antecedent Factors in the Family Histories of 392 Schizophrenics," *American Journal of Psychiatry*, Vol. CX, No. 9 (1954), pp. 668–676.

43 John H. Weakland and Don D. Jackson, "Patient and Therapist Observations on the Circumstances of a Schizophrenic Episode," *American Medical Association Archives of Neurology and Psychiatry*, Vol. LXXIX, No. 4, (1958) pp. 554–574

44. William A. Westley, "Emotionally Healthy Adolescents and Their Family Backgrounds," *The Family in Contemporary Society*, Iago Galdston (ed), International Universities Press, New York, 1958, pp. 131–147.

45. Lyman C. Wynne *et al*, "Psuedo-Mutuality in the Family Relationships of Schizophrenics," *Psychiatry*, Vol. XXI, No. 2, (1958), pp. 205–220.

A Dynamic Frame for the Clinical Approach to Family Conflict

Nathan W. Ackerman

IN THIS PAPER I SHALL offer a dynamic frame within which it may be possible to achieve a clearer understanding of family conflict. With this as background, I shall suggest some general principles for a clinical and therapeutic approach to the resolving of conflict in family relationships.

Conflict and living process are one. From birth to death, living beings move and change continuously. When change occurs, the experience of conflict is inevitable; it is intrinsic to the whole process of human growth and human relations. But the influence of conflict can be catalytic or paralytic; it can integrate or disintegrate human experience. It can enhance human growth and adaptation, or induce its arrest or its distortion. In one aspect, conflict is functional expression of growth and of the changing constellation of adaptive needs; in another, conflict—its vicissitudes, its control, and its ultimate fate—molds the processes of growth. Viewed in this way, human conflict becomes a main point of reference for understanding the forces that bring about adaptation to life and the associated tendencies to health and illness.

The epitome of all human conflict is conflict within the family. It is within the day-by-day intimacies of the family group that conflict exerts its deepest molding force on growth and development and on the related dispositions to health and illness. Conflict in family relations expresses a conflict of values with regard to the goals and functions of family life. It is manifested in competing images and expectations concerning the organization and carrying out of essential family purposes. The purposes and functions of family life are multiple. They have to do with security and survival, sexual union and fulfilment, the care of the young and the aged, the cultivation of a bond of affection and identity, and training for the tasks of social participation. Beyond the prime task of protecting the biological integrity and the growth potential of the offspring, the main ongoing function of the family group is to support the continued socialization and humanization of its members, children and adults alike. When family life fails, the inevitable consequence is a tendency toward dehumanization of behavior.

The Evolving Identity of the Family

The balancing and regulation of these multiple goals and functions constitute a major responsibility. The specific manner in which this is done reflects the unique identity and value constellation of the given family. But establishing the identity and value pattern of the nuclear family group is a continuously evolving process. It is influenced by the representations of the extended family, moving through three or more generations; it is molded from within by the needs and strivings of its members and from without by the sociocultural patterns of the wider community. Society shapes the functions of the family to its own historically emerging goals. The family molds the kinds of persons it requires to carry out these functions. The members themselves, in turn, as far as they can, accommodate the family phenomenon to their respective, individualized needs.

The specific forms of family vary with the culture. In our own rapidly changing, heterogeneous culture, there cannot be a clear uniformity of family pattern. There are, rather, multiple and varied family types and, within this matrix of variability, there is great diversity of family conflicts.

The total configuration of the family molds the forms of behavior that are required in the roles of husband and wife, father and mother, parent and child, child and sibling. Each member adapts according to his unique balance of tendencies to conform or rebel, to submit to or actively alter, the family role expectations.

53

Insofar as this process is a progressively evolving one, the identity and value orientation of the family group changes over the stretch of time. Thus, the relations of individual and group undergo a progressive shift in accordance with advancing stages of family development and also in relation to the individual member's sex, age, family position and role, and personal strivings.

Allegiance to a particular set of identity and value representations forms the patterns for the family's functions, its role adaptations, and the corresponding family alignments. A conflict of identities, values, and strivings brings a rift, a split in the family group which mobilizes one segment against another. Such splits within the family may be horizontal, vertical, or diagonal. They may set male against female, mother and son against father and daughter, the younger generation against the older one. The opposing factions may be equal or severely unequal in power and in composition. It may be two against two, three against one, or one against all the others. It is almost never "all for one and one for all." Occasionally the fragmentation extends to the extreme of each man for himself. The breaking up of the family unit into warring factions distorts the balance of family functions. In a selective manner it favors some family functions, while it disables and warps others.

Conflict in family relations is therefore the functional expression of competing representations of what the family is or ought to be, how it may or may not serve the needs of its members, and how it may or may not fortify their role adaptations both within the family and in the wider community. What the family does or ought to do for its members, male or female, young and old, and what they in turn do for family and community is reflected in the patterns of complementarity of role relations of man and wife, parent and child, parent and grandparent, child and sibling. Such complementarity expresses in action the implicit identity and value orientation of the particular family.

Competition and Co-operation

The balancing and regulation of these multiple family functions are best carried out in an emotional climate of understanding and co-operation. But competition and co-operation in family relations are not necessarily opposites. Under favorable circumstances, certain transitional competitive trends may be the means to achievement of new levels of union and co-operation. Competition may have healthy or pathogenic effects. It may lead to new levels of identity and sharing in family relations or it may aggravate a tendency to emotional alienation and fragmentation of relationships. Whether it does one or the other depends upon the dynamic context of a particular conflict within the larger frame of the dynamic evolution of the family as a whole. In the larger concatenation of family events, what is competition at one phase in the development in the relations of man and wife, or parent and child, may become co-operation in a later phase and vice versa.

Conflict in family life occurs at multiple levels. From outside inward, there may be conflict between the surrounding community and the family, or between representatives of the extended family entity and the nuclear family unit. There may also be conflict between one segment of the nuclear family and another, or between particular family members. And, finally, there may be conflict within the mind of an individual member. Insofar as the family is an open behavior system, conflict constitutes a potent contagious force. It invades and pervades every aspect of family experience. Conflict at any one level influences conflict at every other level. The feedback of influence among these several levels of conflict is circular and interpenetrating.

But conflict and the means of coping with it constitute a single dynamic process. Conflict and the corresponding coping devices are an inseparable unit; one cannot talk of the one without referring to the other. The end results of conflict with respect to adaptation, and the vicissitudes of sickness and health, depend fully as much on the means implemented for the control of conflict as on the content of conflict itself. The organization of the family's resources for the control of conflict, both conscious and unconscious, expresses the unceasing struggle to enhance family role complementarity. This struggle involves the interplay between the image of self and the image of family, the accommodation of the needs of individual and group, the interplay between individual defense against anxiety and family group defense against a threat to the

55

continuity and stability of family identity, values, and the corresponding functions. Conflict of this kind tends to become attached to presumed differences of individual identity and personal striving among the family members.

The Struggle for Control

Conflict and its control may be delineated at the three main levels: between family and community, between the minds of family members, and within the mind of any one member. Conflict in family relations may be solved, or it may be contained; it may be compensated, or the attempt at compensation may fail. The outcome of the struggle for control may be stated in the following alternatives:

1. The conflict is correctly perceived, and an early and rational solution is found.

2. The conflict is correctly perceived, and is contained while an effective solution, not immediately available, is being sought.

3. The conflict is misperceived or distorted; it is not adequately compromised; it is neither effectively contained nor adequately compromised, and spills over into irrational "acting out"

4. The control of conflict fails and the failure leads to progressive disorganization of family relations.

The effectivness of control of conflict depends on clear and accurate perception of the nature of the conflict. In the last analysis, such perception is a shared function, an expression of a particular quality of complementarity of family role relations. In an ultimate sense, no one person by himself can achieve the needed clarity of perception, nor move from there to the implementation of effective control. This process is fundamentally a function of family interaction.

The pattern of conflict may be appropriate or inappropriate to the prevailing family problems. It may be rational or irrational. It may have a central or peripheral significance to the inner life of the family. It may be dormant or overt, conscious or unconscious, diffuse or circumscribed; it may be benign or malignant, reversible or irreversible. In family process, one conflict may be substituted for another, or the pathogenic focus of conflict may be displaced from one part of the family to another. In a parallel sense, attempts at control may be appropriate or inappropriate, rational or irrational, strong or weak. The dominant pattern of complementarity in family role relations influences the selection of individual defenses against anxiety, such as denial, projection, displacement, withdrawal, and so on. At the level of group defense, there may be an increased rigidification of role patterns, an exaggerated loosening of these patterns, mechanization and routinization of family relations, increased emotional distance, thinning and distortion of communication, recourse to diversion and escape, indulgence in prejudice and "acting out" in which all or several members of the family participate.

The adaptive attempts to contain and control the effects of conflicts often take the form of compromise. Such compromise may be rational or irrational. Irrational compromise fosters "acting out." The greater the irrationality, the greater the cost in terms of misfits in family role relations and of impairment in the emotional health of the family members. In irrational compromise, one part of the family is protected, while another part suffers injury. The inevitable consequence is further distortion in the emotional life of the family, with new conflicts superimposed upon the old.

Of special importance is the emergence of injurious patterns of prejudice and scapegoating which appear to fortify one part of the family at the expense of another. The scapegoating may victimize a family pair or a particular individual; the victim may be a child, an adolescent, or an adult. The effects of such prejudice and scapegoating are of fundamental significance, with regard to the unconscious selection of one or another member as the victim of emotional breakdown and mental illness. In some families this destructive influence is mitigated in some measure by the unconscious selection of one member to provide a counterbalancing protective support, in effect to function in the role of "family healer."

Interpersonal and Intrapersonal Conflict

A central concern for the clinician must be the connections between interpersonal conflict in family relations and intrapersonal conflict within the mind of one member. When family conflict is sopped up and internalized, when it becomes locked inside the mind of one person, it cannot be solved. If a useful and healthful solution is to be found, intrapsychic conflict must be activated and reprojected into the field of family interaction. Unless this is done, the submerged conflict becomes entrenched, isolated, and leads progressively to distortion and new conflict. In other words, the longer the period of intrapsychic containment and isolation from the field of active interpersonal interchange, the less probable it is that the pathogenic trend can be reversed.

Conflict between the minds of family members and conflict within the mind of any one member stand in reciprocal relation to one another. The two levels of conflict constitute a circular feedback system. Interpersonal conflict in family relations affects intrapsychic conflict and vice versa. Generally speaking, interpersonal conflict in the family group precedes the establishment of fixed patterns of intrapsychic conflict. Psychopathic distortion and symptom formation are a late product of the process of internalization of persistent and pathogenic forms of family conflict. Potentially, these disturbances are reversible if the intrapsychic and symptom-producing conflict can once more be externalized; that is, if it can be reprojected into the field of family interaction, where a new solution can be found. If, on the other hand, the conflict remains locked within the individual's mind, the resulting pathology becomes progressively fixed and irreversible.

A fuller appreciation of the role of conflict in family dynamics is possible only within the frame of a general theory of the homeostasis of family behavior. In this sense, the vicissitudes of conflict must be examined in two dimensions, the longitudinal and the cross-sectional. In the longitudinal dimension the main patterns of conflict and the corresponding coping devices can be traced as these are passed down through three generations. In the cross-section, it is important to define the central conflicts within the family group as it is now constituted and the resources that are mobilized to deal with these conflicts.

In this way, the efficacy of coping with conflict and the adaptative performance of family over a defined period of time can be assessed in relation to the fulfilment of the family's aims and values, regulation of its essential function, and the resulting balance of health and illness. It is to be borne in mind that, as the family evolves from one stage to the next, it integrates and equilibrates in a special way its multiple purposes—biological survival, individuation, sexual differentiation, socialization, and creative development. As the family moves progressively through each phase of its life cycle, from early marriage before the advent of children to early parenthood with the first child, and from then on through advancing stages of parenthood with increasing numbers of children, a changing constellation of family conflicts emerges. It is this evolutionary configuration of complex, interwoven processes that defines the growth potential of the given family. Family as family cannot stay the same; it moves forward or backward. In the last analysis, it is the pattern of coping with conflict that influences the relative balance between the tendency to cling to the old and the urge to receive new experience. In this way, the control of conflict affects the family's capacity for growth. When the control of conflict fails or is decompensated, the excess of anxiety induces a more intense clinging to what is old and reduces the ability to learn from new experience. The trend, therefore, is toward great fixity and stereotypy of behavior and a constriction of growth.

The inevitable consequence of this reduction of growth potential is a distorted balance of family functions, a rigidification and warping of some, and a disproportionate focus on others. In the extreme, one basic family function may be sacrificed to another. Sexual fulfilment may be sacrificed to child-rearing and vice-versa. The incentive for maturation and creative expansion may be subordinated to the need for omnipotent protection and static security. Affection, spontaneous expression, and pleasure may be suppressed in the interest of fortifying authority and discipline. The personal needs of the member may be sacrificed to the striving for social conformity, and so on. All such trends are reflected in the shifting pattern of complementarity of family role relations.

The Diagnostic Task

The task of family diagnosis is to establish the specific dynamic relations between the balance of tendencies to health and illness in a given family type and the parallel tendency of the group to maintain emotional health in its members or induce in them special forms of psychiatric disablement. In the field of psychopathology, we search out this very specificity of relations between family psychopathology and individual psychopathology. In disturbed families, no matter when we intervene, it is possible to detect and to define certain ongoing pathogenic conflicts. It should be remembered that the pathogenic forces of family life that originally contributed to psychiatric breakdown in one or more individual members continue to assert themselves in the present configuration of family conflict, even though they may now be structured and expressed in a different way. At the point of professional intervention, it is essential to trace the interplay between these pathogenic family conflicts and the conflicts that have become deposited in the intrapsychic life of one or more disabled members.

In our studies of family process at the Jewish Family Service we endeavor to classify family types according to their mental health potentials. We are seeking ways of establishing parallel diagnostic definitions of disturbed functioning in the family group and disturbed functioning in the family member. We attempt to correlate certain types of family identity, role complementarity, conflict patterns, and disturbances of family development with the emergence of one or another form of psychiatric illness in the individual member. We are trying to learn something of the dynamic correlation between family and individual behavior in three broad categories of disturbance: schizophrenia, neurosis, and character disorder.

Without dilating on this aspect of our studies, I may say in passing that there are to be found certain common features in all sick families, also significant differences. In all three groups, there are disturbances in growth, varying patterns of prejudice, scapegoating, the victimization of particular parts of the family, and compensatory healing functions. Among these family types, however, are critical differences in the quality of impairment of the growth capacity of the family, also in the patterns of prejudice scapegoating, and healing. This variety is very evident in differences in family identity, in value orientation in the content of conflict, and in the patterns of coping with conflicts, which are transmitted through three generations.

60

Families as families seem to get stuck at different points of the growth curve. Some are fixed at the level of concern with sheer biological survival. Others seem to get fixed at the level of problems of individuation in the family members. Still others are predominantly preoccupied with issues of sexual differentiation. Only rarely are these families mainly absorbed with questions of nourishing the creative development of the members. Now and then one encounters a family in which there is a peculiar merging of concerns with sheer biological survival of one part of the family while there is also absorption with the creative nourishment of another part of the family.

The Family Therapist

In other reports,[1] I have described the specific characteristics of the psychotherapeutic process with the family group. I believe that the social structuring of a therapeutic interview with an entire family group offers a unique kind of challenge. Therefore, the role of a family therapist assumes a form that is distinct from the role of the psychotherapist in a more conventional mode of treatment, whether it be psychoanalysis, individual psychotherapy of other types, or group psychotherapy with an artificially composed group of patients who come together for the first time to be treated by the same therapist. I should like here merely to highlight the more outstanding and relatively unique functions of the role of the family therapist.

Under this plan, regardless of the nature of the presenting complaint and regardless of the fact that one family member is pre-

[1] Nathan W. Ackerman, *The Psychodynamics of Family Life*, Basic Books, New York, 1958; "Toward an Integrative Therapy of the Family," *American Journal of Psychiatry*, Vol. CXIV, No. 8 (1958), pp. 727–733; "The Psychoanalytic Approach to the Family," *Science and Psychoanalysis, Vol. II. Individual and Family Dynamics*, Jules H. Masserman, (ed), Grune and Stratton, New York, 1959, pp. 105-211, "Theory of Family Dynamics," *Psychoanalysis and The Psychoanalytic Review*, Winter 1959–1960. Vol. XLVI, No 4, pp. 33–49; "Transference and Counter-Transference," *Psychoanalysis and The Psychoanalytic Review*, Fall 1959. Vol. XLVI, No. 3, pp. 17-28, "Family-focused Therapy of Schizophrenia," *The Out-Patient Treatment of Schizophrenia*, (Sam C. Scher and Howard R. Davis, eds.), Grune and Stratton, New York, 1960, pp. 156–173; "Psychotherapy with the Family Group," *Science and Psychoanalysis*, Vol. IV, Jules Masserman (ed.), Grune and Stratton, New York, 1961, pp. 150–156, "The Emergence of Family Psychotherapy on the Present Scene," *Ten Psychotherapies*, I. Stein (ed). Free Press, Glencoe, Ill. Spring 1961.

sumed to be "the sick one," the entire family group is asked to come to the interview. The unit of interview is the entire group of persons that constitutes a psychic entity. Usually the group includes the nuclear family and certainly all the persons living under one roof. It may also involve additional persons—a grandmother, an aunt, a maid, or even a homemaker—if these persons play a significant role in the ongoing life of the family unit. In other words, significant relatives or other persons may be included in the functional family unit, even though they may reside in another home. In essence, the unit of interview comprises those persons who are part of the functional representation of the family group.

In a first contact with a troubled family, it seems preferable to begin in a fresh unprejudiced way, without prepared historical data obtained separately from individual family members. Experience suggests that a fresh contact with a disturbed family group tends, during the period of treatment, to provide the necessary and relevant historical information. Often such data turn out to be more accurate than material obtained from individual interviews. What goes on between people's minds within the family group can be directly correlated with what goes on inside the mind of one member. As the family wrestles with its immediate distress, relevant fragments of history are injected into the proceedings, and the validity of these disclosures undergoes prompt consensual validation among the family members. Each such revelation tends to be checked by other family members. Thus, reality testing emerges at the outset.

Generally such troubled families are in pain. The family functions are variably disabled, but the family cannot tell the therapist exactly what is wrong. The members are distressed, baffled, and confused, but they cannot at the outset define the nature of the disturbance. They want therapeutic intervention, but they cannot explain clearly what is wrong or what should be done to make it right.

In the family interview process, what one parent conceals, the other reveals. What the parents together hide, the child exposes. What one member expresses in a twisted and prejudiced way is corrected by another. When the anxiety exceeds a certain critical threshold, the family members may enter a silent pact against disclosure of conflict-filled material. Sooner or later, however, such collective denials and conspiracies of silence are broken through—the cat comes out of the bag. Family life by its very nature is inimical to the guarding of privacy. The outcome is contingent on the spontaneous tendency of the family members themselves to stir revelation of hidden family conflicts, and also on the active role of the clinician in catalyzing the release of these deeper experiences. It is incumbent upon the psychotherapist to make a clear distinction between the protection of valid and healthy forms of privacy and the reinforcement of pathogenic forms of privacy. The clinician may in good conscience penetrate those emotional barriers in family communication which maintain pathogenic "secrets."

The clinician strives to reach an understanding with the group as to what is wrong, and how to go about correcting it. In the interview process he moves immediately into the arena of the family's living as it struggles with its current problems. The emphasis is on the immediate distress of the group, the tensions of family relations, the conflicts and the functional disablements here and now.

The therapist enters the family as an active participant. He is taken into the fold as a sort of older relative—perhaps a grandparent—endowed with special powers and wisdom concerning family affairs. All members of the family respond to the therapist both in a real way and in terms of transference projection, but each family member expresses the transference expectations toward the therapist in a different way. The intervention of the therapist into the family phenomenon is somewhat analogous to a chemical process. He enters the family as a kind of chemical reagent, a kind of catalyst or hormone. The family and its various parts combine with and again separate from selected elements of the therapist's identity in accordance with their need and their means of coping with conflict.

The therapist stirs spontaneous interaction among the family members and with himself. He mobilizes an alive and meaningful interchange. He stirs a quality of empathy and intercommunication that is best described as a "touching" experience. In emotional terms, he touches them and invites them to touch him. The family members then come into better touch with one another. The therapist penetrates the pathogenic barriers to closeness and sharing in family relations. He cuts through levels of mistrust, despair, fear, and hatred. He challenges the existing patterns of alienation and fragmentation of family relationships. He questions the necessity for the splits and the warring factions in the family group. He energizes emotional release of conflict-ridden material; he mobilizes action and reaction. He activates awareness of new avenues of sharing, new kinds of intimacy, new levels of identification, and realignment of family relations.

In so doing the therapist makes deliberate and discretionary use of the nonverbal aspects of intercommunication. In order to facilitate this process he may, according to his own clinical discretion, call pointed attention to facial expression, body postures, movements, and so on. By these means he expands and sharpens the perception of relevant family conflicts. He undercuts the more pathogenic defenses against anxiety and helps the family members to discover healthier ones. In order to bring this about, he must particularly pierce the hypocritical, righteous, self-justifying forms of defense. He must challenge unreal and impossible demands, fruitless and vindictive forms of blaming, and omnipotent destructive invasions by one member into the life of another.

Of central importance in this connection is the therapist's responsibility for counteracting the more malignant forms of scapegoating in family relations. Through his intervention he facilitates a shift in the object of the pathogenic destructive invasion. The destructive conflict is moved away from the scapegoated victim back to its original source in the family group—usually some covert and unsolved conflict between the parents. He offers support for the family member who most needs it, the weaker one or the one under immediate attack.

In these proceedings, the therapist is continuously alert to the subtly shifting focus of the center of pathogenic conflict from one part of the family to another. Whenever the conflict becomes sharply pointed, he energizes an expanding awareness of the interrelations between interpersonal and intrapsychic conflict.

Through his use of self the therapist injects something new into the emotional life of the family—new kinds of emotions and new kinds of perception of family relations, pointing toward the solution of conflict, healthier compensation, and more effective reality testing. By these means he encourages an increased mutuality of need satisfaction and the discovery of new levels of intimacy, sharing, support, and identity which open the way to new growth in family relations.

Pinpointing the Central Conflicts

The aim of the clinician must be to delineate the central conflicts of the family group and the resulting disturbances in complementarity of role adaptation. The conflicts and corresponding role disturbances at the several significant levels must be defined as to their intensity, their lability, and their location within the life space of the family. Within the patterns of contemporary conflict, one traces the components of pathogenic influences which have come up from the past. One must appraise the family's resources for the solution, containment, and compensation of conflict so as to promote and maintain health. In this connection it is of crucial importance to discern the dynamic relations between individual defense against anxiety and family group defense against a threat to the continuity of its functions.

The aims of the clinician with respect to family conflict are:

1. To help the family achieve a clearer and sharper definition of the real content of conflict. This is done by dissolving the disguises of conflict and resulting confusions in family relationships. A greater accuracy of perception of family conflict is the goal.

2. To energize dormant interpersonal conflicts, bringing them overtly into the live processes of family interaction, thus making them accessible to solution.

3. To lift concealed intrapsychic conflict to the level of interpersonal relations, where it may be coped with more effectively.

4 To counteract inappropriate displacements of conflict.

5. To neutralize the irrational prejudices and scapegoating which are involved in the displacement of conflict. The purpose here is to put the conflict back where it came from in family role relations, that is, to reattach it to its original source, and attempt to work it out there, so as to counteract the trend toward prejudi-

cial assault and disparagement of any one member. The aim is to relieve an excessive burden of conflict on one victimized part of the family, either an individual or a family pair, and at the same time to ease the load on the family member who fulfils the role of family healer.

6. To activate an improved level of complementarity in family role relations.

Treatment Techniques

The specific techniques of family psychotherapy have been demonstrated with a sound-film recording of a family group in treatment. The value of such recordings of the family interview process is self-evident. Seeing is believing. The written word, regardless of the measure of descriptive skills, cannot possibly convey the live quality of a therapeutic interview; it cannot give a faithful picture of the sequence of events. Nor is a tape recording of vocal expression much more satisfactory. Too much of the essence is lost. By contrast, a sound-film record of the therapeutic family interview process is perhaps the closest approach to an optimal study procedure. It is the only method that provides a Gestalt, a merging of the image of face, voice, emotion, and bodily expression. It reveals action and reaction in accurate sequence. It provides a suitable instrument for the systematic study of the relations between what goes on inside the mind and what goes on between minds. It is therefore a useful medium for the illumination of the dynamics of therapeutic interaction.

For several years at the Jewish Family Service we have been filming family interviews as part of an ongoing study of the problems of family diagnosis and family treatment. The moving-picture studies constitute one method in a range of procedures for obtaining the relevant data. Other procedures include psychiatric examination, psychological tests, home visits; the integration of psychotherapy of the family group with the social techniques of treatment of family problems and family life education. The data gathered by these various means are organized through the use of systematic schedules, so as to obtain comparable data on a range of family types

At the present time, we are in process of evolving specific research designs for the evaluation of sound-film records of family interaction process. We are devising multiple methods of evaluation: (1) psychodynamic evaluation by the clinician; (2) spontaneous evaluation of the interview events by the family group viewing its own films; (3) interactional analysis by the Bales method; [2] (4) a special study of family identity and values; (5) a special study of agreement, disagreement, and coalitions in family relations; (6) a special study of the relations of prejudice and scapegoating to problems of family mental health, and a parallel investigation of the role of the family healer.

[2] Robert F. Bales, *Interaction Process Analysis,* Addison-Wesley Press, Cambridge, Mass , 1950

A Casework Approach to Disturbed Families

Celia Mitchell

SOCIAL CASEWORK as a social science concerned with the institution of the family has had a relatively brief history. Originating in the charity organization movement, social work was first animated by a concern for those families who were casualties of the socio-economic conditions resulting from the industrial revolution. The revolution in methods of production was accompanied by vast changes in the total social structure including deep and far-reaching changes in the structure of the family. Patterns of adaptation suitable to earlier family forms became obsolescent, and the family was confronted by the necessity of learning new modes of adaptation.

As psychoanalytic insights began to infiltrate the practice of social work, the emphasis on social forces was joined by an emphasis on understanding both individual personality and the family in which and by which it is shaped. A little more than half a century ago, the professionalization of social work practice began in earnest with the establishment of schools of social work, and with the formalization of theory and methodology essential to a scientifically-based endeavor.

Casework Principles

The core of casework interest has always been the individual or family in need of help because of a breakdown in social functioning. Basic to casework is the belief that conflicts between individuals can usually be resolved to the benefit of each; and that when

68

this is not possible, confrontation of the client with this reality may lead to new alignments in relationship and functioning. From the outset, casework theory has asserted that the family of the individual client, both the family of origin and the created family, is significant in the etiology, development, and outcome of individual conflict and adaptation. Even when the typical treatment process involved only one member of the family, caseworkers adhered to a family-oriented emphasis. In 1944, Dr. Gomberg stressed the specific function of the family agency in these terms: ". . . a determinative focus for family casework does exist in the seemingly obvious but overlooked fact that a family agency, as differentiated from any other, is intended to deal with the problems which primarily concern the *family as a whole.*" [1]

The client-worker relationship as an enabling, motivating, and growth-promoting force is a basic component of casework practice. The special characteristics of the casework relationship came under intensified scrutiny when family casework agencies extended their services to include not only clients with situational reality problems but also those revealing all types of intrapsychic, intrafamilial, interpersonal, and social maladaptations. This type of service, which has increasingly become identified with casework, is sometimes referred to as counseling—a term introduced to highlight the psychological orientation of casework treatment as differentiated from its traditionally environmental approach. This shift in emphasis does not imply an abandonment of responsibility for the social aspects of individual and family malfunction, but rather an expansion of the caseworker's responsibility and skill. Whatever designation is used, the characteristic casework approach is the synthesis of all the relevant components (social-psychological, somatic, and cultural) in the human situations it confronts and influences through its intervention.

To this end, the profession of casework has intensively combed psychological theories, medical knowledge, anthropological discoveries, societal processes, and other related concepts and tech-

[1] M. Robert Gomberg, "The Specific Nature of Family Case Work," in *A Functional Approach to Family Case Work,* Jessie Taft (ed.), University of Pennsylvania Press, Philadelphia, 1944, p. 113.

niques relevant to the development of casework theory and methodology. In only a few decades, casework has moved from providing charity for the indigent to a systematic effort to prevent or repair all types of individual and family distress and breakdown. It has used techniques designed to strengthen ego capacity, to confront and resolve conflict and maladaptation, and to promote the maturational process. It has moved from "improving the condition of the poor" to charging a fee for casework service. The most recent step in the progression has been the emergence of the private practice of casework.[2] At present, caseworkers offer a vast range of services to help individuals and families in every type of predicament. They also function in ancillary, collaborative, or consultant capacities to implement the work of other professions under other than casework auspices. Under casework auspices the services of related professions and available community agencies have always been utilized. The aim of casework is to mobilize all the resources necessary for effective help. Regardless of the setting in which it is performed, casework is focused on the effects of crisis or breakdown in the individual and the family, with a view to removing the obstacles to restored and improved functioning.

Use of Sociological Concepts in Assessing Functioning

In recent years the casework profession has embarked on interdisciplinary research, with the aim of testing and validating its hypotheses, methods, and results. Sometimes scientifically trained sociologists have been employed on agency staffs, or caseworkers have worked in special projects with sociologists, anthropologists, and social psychologists. More recently the profession has completed a curriculum study—a stock-taking that represents another nodal point in its maturation.[3] The findings of this study are bound to have important consequences for training and practice in social work in the second half of the century that saw its beginning professionalization during the first half.

[2] See Ruth Fizdale, "Formalizing the Relationship Between Private Practitioners and Social Agencies," *Social Casework*, Vol. XL, No. 10 (1959), pp. 539–544. Carl M. Shafer, "The Family Agency and the Private Casework Practitioner," *Social Casework*, Vol. XL, No 10 (1959), pp. 531–538.

[3] *Social Work Curriculum Study*, 13 Volumes, Werner W. Boehm (ed.), Council on Social Work Education, New York, 1959.

Increasingly, caseworkers have had to recognize that their theoretical and methodological equipment for understanding and helping the individual is not adequate for understanding and treating the family as an entity. In the past decade, sociological studies of family structure and function, of family processes and roles, have seemed to offer new dimensions for such an understanding, and the terminology of sociology has been used increasingly in casework gatherings and literature, in formal co-existence with psychoanalytically-derived concepts and descriptions. The danger of imitating the sociologist's orientation, when what was urgently needed was integration, began to be manifested. The same danger had originally existed in the use of psychoanalytic concepts. There was also the tendency to deal separately with these two levels of abstraction, the psychological and the social— ". . . more an expression of our own perceptual and integrative limitations than a result of any inherent dichotomy between more or less internal and external phenomena." [4]

Manifestly, the choice and range of social roles adopted by the individual, the assignment of roles in a family, role complementarity, and success and failure in carrying roles are intertwined with the intrapsychic dynamics of the individual as these develop in response to intrafamilial and interpersonal experiences. It is also apparent that the utilization of the concept of role functioning in diagnosis and treatment offers additional advantages, when dynamically based. The most frequently experienced concern of clients is *precisely* in relation to anxiety or dissatisfaction about the role performance of one or more members of the family. In addition, certain aspects of role function as well as certain types of roles may either enhance or damage individual adaptation in accordance with their dynamic significance.

Similar considerations are in order when changes in role or the assumptions of new roles in family relationships occur as a result of therapeutic intervention. When efforts are made to shift the balance in family relations, for example, in a marital pair such as the monotonously recurrent "aggressive wife" and "passive husband," the practitioner has to be sure that the goal expresses the

[4] Celia Brody Mitchell, "Family Interviewing in Family Diagnosis," *Social Casework*, Vol. XL, No 7 (1959), pp. 381–384.

desire and capacity of the individuals concerned and is not simply the practitioner's value judgment dressed up in psychological terms. Is such an effort calculated to strengthen or further to weaken the marital relationship? If it is an appropriate goal, what sequence of psychological events is prerequisite to its pursuit? Or, to take another example of an equally common type of family pair, the parent-child pair consisting of a compulsive, controlling mother, and a passive, constricted child, of what avail is it to the child to stimulate the expression of his aggression, unless both mother and child are prepared by the treatment process to absorb this change in his behavior? Even so, is it not questionable to view the mother-child conflict apart from the marital partnership that has eventuated in this particular type of mother-child pair? Such a procedure may result in the family boat's springing more leaks than it already has.

An approach that takes the family as family into account permits the practitioner to examine significant pair relationships, to assess individual family members, and to regard all these elements as equally important, not as separate or competing considerations. Intervention into one individual's functioning or into one area of family process has ramifications for the whole family group and its total functioning. This is a paramount casework principle, as is its corollary—that appropriate intervention at one point can, like a pebble thrown into a lake, stir widening ripples with far-reaching results.

Family Diagnosis and Treatment

The trouble has been, as I have already mentioned, that the theory underlying casework practice with individuals has not been supplemented with the methodological equipment necessary for the understanding and treatment of the *family constellation*. It is an interesting phenomenon—supplying grist for the sociologist's mill—that studies and experimentation on the family as a group and on family pairs, conducted by psychiatrists, psychoanalysts, caseworkers, and anthropologists, have been reported in the literature only recently.[5] Caseworkers have begun to seek new opera-

[5] Readers are referred to the bibliography in another article in this volume, p 49.

tional hypotheses on the basis of their own experience and have also extrapolated related concepts from the findings reported by other professions.[6]

Dr. Gomberg's paper, written in 1957, was a trail-blazing paper In it he observed:

> Existing clinical diagnostic tools and classifications focus exclusively on individual personality. Our attempt in casework to encompass the larger whole, to include the social factors and the family in our diagnosis, is only partially successful. No diagnostic or conceptual system exists which describes, assesses, or classifies the family configuration, yet this is clearly needed if the diagnosis of the individual is not to be in a vacuum but rather within the context of the social and emotional environment in which he lives, adjusts, suffers, fails, or succeeds. We must not choose between a concept of the family and a psychology of the individual; it is through a balanced understanding of the interrelatedness between the two that we can achieve the most meaningful understanding and the most effective treatment.[7]

In this paper he referred also to the activities of Dr. Ackerman during the preceding twenty years that antedated the recent intensification of interest and activity in the area of family dynamics for the purpose of evolving a theoretical system for family diagnosis and treatment.

A major break-through occurred with the publication of Dr. Ackerman's book in 1958.[8] In this book he offered a comprehensive theoretical approach in which the emerging personality of the individual is related to the family configuration. He presented a systematic scheme for organizing and correlating data on the family group with data on individual family members. This scheme encompassed bio-psycho-social factors, patterns of communication, control of conflict, mechanisms for restitution, extrafamilial social roles, pathogenic conflicts, strivings and values, capacity to accommodate to new experiences, reality testing, learning and growth. The medium through which this type of family diagnosis is de-

[6] Viola W. Weiss and Russell R. Monroe, "A Framework for Understanding Family Dynamics: Parts I and II," *Social Casework*, Vol. XL, Nos. 1 and 2 (1959), pp 3–9; 80–87.

[7] M. Robert Gomberg, "Family Diagnosis· Trends in Theory and Practice," *Social Casework*, Vol. XXXIX, Nos. 2–3 (1958), p. 73

[8] Nathan W. Ackerman, *The Psychodynamics of Family Life*, Basic Books, New York, 1958.

veloped is the family session, which enables the family practitioner better to understand and appraise the current family situation, find the clues to the reason for the breakdown in adaptation, and gather significant data concerning the dynamic evolution of the family by *direct observation* of the total group.

In viewing family interaction, the practitioner is able to get a picture of the conflicts, adaptation, and self-image of each individual family member, as well as the manner in which he relates himself to others in the family. This procedure rounds out the interviewing process which, for the purposes both of diagnosis and of treatment, had heretofore depended almost exclusively upon the individual session, with occasional resort to joint interviewing or home visits. The established pattern has been to gather data about family relations, individual by individual, and then to formulate a working family diagnosis on which to base a plan of treatment by correlating these data. Because of its emotional immediacy, the family session provides opportunities for therapeutic intervention in the interaction that is taking place which are not afforded by merely talking about what has already happened. The family session also provides clues to the appropriate timing of therapeutic intervention in specific family-pair conflicts as well as clues to entrenched personal conflicts that require individual attention. By using a combination of techniques in a flexible manner, the therapist can respond to the uniqueness of family patterns as well as to individual needs.

Problems Posed by Family Interviewing

It is important to underscore the assertion that family interviewing neither excludes nor is in opposition to individual treatment, but rather it is concerned with family interactional processes. At the same time it provides an added level of insight into and treatment of the individual family members—the family level. In either case, the decision to use individual, pair, or family sessions and the integrated use of these sessions in whatever combination will depend upon dynamic considerations and goals.

Theory and methodology, however sound, are one thing; the ability to put them into practice is another. Inadequate preparation for, or the premature undertaking of, family interviewing is bound to result in poor performance It is essential that the practitioner who attempts to do it have specific training, experience, and supervision in the use of this technique, yet the availability of this type of experience is still pathetically meager. Nevertheless, the whole question of family therapy and the role of the family practitioner—whether in casework or psychiatry—cannot be postponed. As the schizophrenic nightmare of the destruction of the world has become a real possibility, anxiety, stress, and family disturbances can be expected to spiral at an ever faster rate.

Many have taken pause at the problems involved in assuming the role of family practitioner and the accompanying increase in anxiety and stress experienced in attempting to meet multiple and conflicting demands. These are real problems that must be dealt with at all levels of training, supervision, and personal preparation, and that can be mastered in time. The fact that serious problems exist, however, is not a sound reason for reluctance to take on this responsibility.

Some critics have pointed out that casework lacks a family typology, and that, therefore, we are at a disadvantage in undertaking family treatment. Is it not reasonable to hypothesize that a family typology may be developed more quickly and accurately when we work with the family group than when we approach the family as an aggregate of individuals? Unfortunately there is no way in which we can formulate a family typology apart from actual practice and research into practice. Practice and research can, in turn, help clarify the issue of the types of intervention most beneficial to certain types of families. The recent book by Reiner and Kaufman [9] makes an important contribution to this problem by presenting a classification of parental pathology in relation to a major social disorder—delinquency. The authors indicate their concern with filling "one of the major gaps in the spectrum of psychotherapy." However, as they themselves point out, they omit certain important facets of the problem of delinquency when they limit their discussion to its clinical aspects. They refer with regret "to the awkwardness of descriptive phrases that tend to be de-

[9] Beatrice Simcox Reiner and Irving Kaufman, *Character Disorders in Parents of Delinquents*, Family Service Association of America, New York, 1959.

humanizing." The importance of this contribution only serves to emphasize the enormous gap between what is needed and what remains to be done in synthesizing all the relevant factors that comprise or affect any human entity.

In still other quarters there is a demand for appropriate criteria to be used in selecting family treatment as the method of choice. This demand, although theoretically valid, is made even before sufficient experience has been accumulated to warrant the establishment of criteria by which to judge its usefulness and its limitations. This is contrary to any scientific procedure that must depend on actual experimentation. Others have cited the complexities of family treatment and the difficulties currently faced by caseworkers who have been oriented to work with individuals. Otto Pollak, for example, has written:

> Persons with a psychological orientation traditionally have directed attention to the single individual. To understand pluralities in psychological terms demands a tremendous increase in observations and, in the analysis of these observations, an increase in integrative effort. In family agencies the shift from a psychologically oriented concern with individuals to a similar concern with groups, therefore, imposes a great burden on the caseworker and on the psychiatric consultant.[10]

This is a fair appraisal of the complexities of the problem, but the complexities should not deter us from attempting to find more effective ways of solving the problems of unhappy family life. The social urgency represented by the alarming increase in the number of disturbed families should join forces with professional ingenuity for the purpose of discovering improved methods of treatment.

Values of Family Treatment

Basic to the premises underlying the acceptance of family treatment as a valuable method is that the establishment of personal identity and the choice of neurosis and defenses are largely determined by the person's experiences in his family. Sometimes concurrent individual and family intervention are required. When family treatment is provided under casework auspices, the family

---

[10] Otto Pollak, "Family Diagnosis: Commentary," *Social Casework*, Vol. XXXIX, No. 2-3 (1958), p. 83.

caseworker has to serve as the integrative force in the treatment plan—mobilizing, co-ordinating, and equilibrating all the auxiliary services necessary to implement the casework process. In disturbed families, the parents' difficulties in giving and receiving love, affection, and support can lead to a failure to fulfil their parental roles, with the result that the children are either neglected, placed in the parental role, or used as scapegoats. Since a person's socialization is dependent on his receiving benign doses of both love and authority, insufficient or incorrect amounts of either can result in his making distorted or disproportionate claims on his marital partner, his children, or on other persons. In some families, the parents' entrenched immaturity results in chronic crises, disorganization, and misery. The vulnerability of these individuals makes the adult roles they are forced to assume overwhelming in the demands placed on them. The predicaments they are unable to avoid in turn give rise to new troubles. These fragile families require long-term or even lifetime help on a recurrent basis.

When the caseworker intervenes in such a situation he becomes the social parent. If he can assume this role without ambivalence and without an unspoken demand for reward in the form of rapid or substantial change, he can introduce order, help establish improved patterns of communication, and reduce feelings of helplessness. As a consequence, hostility is decreased and self-esteem is raised. In many instances, the gains made, although they take place slowly, can prevent or ameliorate severe psychiatric disorders, delinquent acting out, or the placement of children. As a nurturing authority, the caseworker accepts dependency needs and, at the same time, encourages the family members' moves toward independence. He responds to their expression of feelings and promotes more awareness of the feelings of others, but he sets limits to destructive behavior. He does not merely encourage the ventilation of anger and the discharge of tension but he holds out hope of improvement and the possibility of achieving positive goals. To be effective in this role the worker must have empathy, perceptiveness, flexibility, and responsiveness to changing needs and feelings. Most of all, perhaps, the worker should be able to face honestly all types of feelings, including his own. It is extraordinarily difficult to fulfil this delicate role. On the other hand, there is a special kind of gratification that comes from seeing the family grow emotionally and improve in its relationships, which sustains him in this complex task. More thought needs to be given to methods of maintaining the gains made over long periods of treatment. The family's increased capacity for self-help and direction can be supported by such means as membership in groups that are ego-strengthening and that can prevent the isolation characteristic of many disturbed families.

There are many families that seek and use help with a special problem or at a time of unusual stress, and then can go ahead on their own with greater competence and satisfaction. In these instances, it is extremely important to choose the appropriate level of treatment and to have a clear understanding with the family about the particular aspect of disturbance that will be dealt with.

Benefits of the Family Approach

Some families call for help at a point of extreme stress The family control patterns have broken down and the result is overwhelming fear of uncontrolled violence. For example, one frantic mother pressed the worker to give her an appointment immediately. Her 10-year-old daughter had grown increasingly unmanageable. The urgent telephone call for help was the result of a knife-brandishing scene. Both parents felt unable to cope with the girl, and the implication that the solution was to place her away from home was just below the surface. Their only other child, a 16-year-old boy, as well as various relatives, were also afraid of a catastrophic incident.

The series of family interviews [11] that were initiated upon the heels of this urgent plea, resulted in a lessening of the explosive tension in the family. This was accomplished by the practitioner's assumption of control and the setting of limits on behavior in the family session. For example, the practitioner restrained the girl from dominating the discussion or from leaving the sessions whenever she felt thwarted. Her feeling of omnipotence had mounted

[11] All family sessions described in this paper were conducted by Dr Nathan W. Ackerman as part of a seminar on family diagnosis for the staff of the Family Mental Health Clinic of Jewish Family Service.

in proportion to her parents' impotence. This assumption of authority and control by the practitioner will evoke all types of bribes, threats, and maneuvers which have to be met directly and reliably. An atmosphere has to be created in which the ventilation of feelings of injury and mutual accusations becomes possible as the practitioner removes the threat of annihilation. The practitioner, however, must inject the idea that there is no single culprit and that all must participate in reaching an understanding of the events that led to the crisis in which all are implicated, although they usually are not aware of their involvement. Through the model provided by the practitioner in the sessions, the parent role and the child role become differentiated in the minds of the family members.

No systematic therapy either for parents or for child is possible in a chaotic family situation such as the one described above, until the level of tension has been reduced. In the instance described, the knife-wielding episode turned out to be only a gesture, and the underlying problems that had culminated in this threat of violence began to emerge. In certain types of families in which roles are reversed and the parents look to the children for supplies of love and for support and direction, the practitioner must give repeated demonstration of "emotional feeding" and control before the family can envision the possibilities of improved communication and functioning.

There is another type of family situation that is common in family agencies. Parents call for help with one child, described as "difficult," and are then quick to mention that the other children do not have any problems. In fact they are sometimes described as a source of pride and pleasure, in contrast to the problem child. The usual procedure is for the worker to interview the parents and the problem child. The "good" children are likely to be ignored when in fact they may be in as great or greater trouble than the troublesome child. Then, after the case has been under care for some time, the worker may discover that the true picture is quite different from the one originally presented.

Another common phenomenon is the parents' unconscious "parceling out" of aspects of their own personality among their children. One child is selected to represent the unacceptable part of

79

the parent's personality—the aggressive, the greedy, or the unsuccessful element—while another child has always been the lovable one. Only if the entire family group is seen together, in the process of interacting, can the worker see the actual, rather than the projected, picture. As a result, the worker's entire conceptualization and management of the problem are altered.

In one instance a widow with two boys, 14 and 7, sought help for the older boy. Her complaints against him had overtones of her feeling of being victimized by him. She felt that he needed treatment. Inquiries elicited the information that her life was a struggling lack-luster affair. Her only problem with the younger boy was that she constantly had to protect him from attacks by the older. It was arranged that all three would come for a family session.

In the session, the mother sat between the two boys. The younger one sat so close to her that he was constantly in touch with some part of her body; the older boy sat apart. The mother remained undisturbed by the younger child's constant tugging at her and touching her. Her voice was controlled when she spoke to the older boy whom she criticized for his childishness as well as for his isolation from his peers and his constant solitary TV watching at home. In the course of the interview it developed that the mother had prematurely been given a great deal of responsibility in her own family. She retained an unacknowledged core of rage and depression in her relationship with her own mother that was being transplanted to her relationship with her older son. At the same time she exploited intimacy with the younger child, who was the representation of her unfulfilled baby self still craving for union with the mother. She was oblivious of the gross signs of maturational lag in this boy, as well as of her provocation of the older boy's attacks on the younger by her obvious preference. The family dynamics and the treatment needs of all three were revealed in the session through body gestures and tone of voice as well as in words.

The relief of guilt in the older boy at finding that he was not the only one with a problem or the sole cause of the family distress was of immediate therapeutic importance. The mother's recognition of the "two sides" of her problem made her more available for treatment. Finally, valuable time was gained through the worker's being able to intervene at an early point in the younger child's serious developmental problems.

Interviewing an entire family group offers the advantage of having a number of "observers" who can function as excellent testers of reality for the practitioner. Family members either concur with or contradict each other's perceptions of what is going on. Frequently an unconscious family conspiracy keeps the problem focused on one member and supports communication patterns that suppress real conflicts between other family members. Hence, feelings are manipulated in the service of certain goals and strivings imposed by one parent or both on the entire family. What may then develop is that one of the children acts out the prohibited behavior, is a pariah in the family, and is in danger of becoming delinquent; the other members are models of conformity, but suffer from a loss of spontaneity and individuation.

In one such family both parents and three out of the four children were all hard-working, disciplined, future-oriented people, security-minded and joyless. Their one source of dissatisfaction was the one son, aged 15, whose differences from themselves perplexed and outraged them. They were now frightened as well, since he was doing failing school work and was becoming involved in a delinquent gang. In a series of family sessions their righteousness (particularly in the case of the father, since the mother seemed to be quite detached from the boy) was conspicuous as was their pride in the other three model children. Both parents described the marriage as satisfactory.

In the usual treatment procedure this boy—fat, inarticulate, impulse-ridden, and isolated—would be selected as the client, and one or both parents would be involved for the purposes of support and modification of attitudes where possible. However, the peculiar split in this family's ranks suggested that the compromises they were making in relation to need gratification and repression of rage were not particularly successful, or at least could be maintained only as long as the 15-year-old family scapegoat acted them out. On the other hand, if his acting out went too far, this also would upset the equilibrium.

81

One of the points I wish to make in relation to this family is that a healthy family equilibrium does not require a scapegoat. The objectives of family treatment would be to enable the family ego-alien impulses and needs to be identified and accepted by all the family members rather than projected onto one member. In acknowledging them and dealing with them more successfully, the family would relieve the boy who is the scapegoat of the burden of carrying the unresolved parental problems and he would be in a better position to deal with his own. Furthermore, there would be a better chance of his being admitted into the family circle than if he received individual treatment even if it were fairly successful. A summary of the findings of six exploratory sessions enlarged the perception of the whole family as to the actual problems, placing the problem of the 15-year-old in a totally different perspective and involving all family members in an examination of their needs, their functioning, and their relationships.

In summary, it may be said that the investigation of family dynamics, of family typology, and of treatment aimed at change in family interactional patterns is still in its beginnings. The development of the concept, particularly at this time when the individual, the family, or even the nation in isolation becomes an increasing threat to mental health, holds forth both a challenge and a promise.

Trends Toward Preventive Practice
in Family Service Agencies

Frances L. Beatman

IT IS BECOMING increasingly clear that if social workers are to enhance their understanding of the family and the influences that determine and affect its internal and external identity, they must join forces with persons in the social and behavioral sciences who can help throw light on the complicated phenomena with which social workers deal. The tremendous task involved in undertaking to develop a unitary understanding of the family presents a major challenge to the social work field.

Propelling us toward the accomplishment of the task, however, is the knowledge that the survival of a democratic way of life is dependent on the capacity of families to foster the healthy development of all of their members. Only as we increase our knowledge about the influences that support positive family functioning and those that create family problems, can we refine our methods and programs for helping the family provide its members with the values and attitudes that are necessary in carrying out their life roles.

There is precedent for the hope that, if we are clear about the direction to be taken to enable today's family to become a dependable foundation of our society, programing and implementation can follow. Historically, on a national level, provisions have gradually been made to combat the deteriorating and debilitating ravages of poverty, epidemics, and ignorance. The establishment of health and welfare programs has set a precedent for the inauguration of preventive programs in the field of human relations.

There is no lack of recognition today that "something needs to be done" if the social development of man is to keep pace with the technological and scientific advances of the modern world.

The family holds the key to the transmission of both the values that make for positive mental health and the conflicts that lead to unhappiness and deviant behavior. The question facing society today is how to buttress the family's ability to fulfil its positive possibilities in a highly competitive and mobile society whose values and structures, including the very structure of the family, are undergoing rapid change. Despite the fact that, as a nation, we have many social and economic advantages, the necessity for rapid adaptation has created an upheaval for many individuals, leaving them without moorings. The multiple choices and alternatives open to people in our changing society are doubtless the source of much of the mass anxiety that is evident on every hand. It is not clear, however, to what extent present patterns of behavior and changing goals and values are really a cover for underlying mass anxiety and to what extent they represent positive, healthy strivings.

These problems of social adjustment are not indigenous to particular social or economic groups. Neither are they a temporary manifestation of some radical social change in the lives of a special group. Although families recently arrived in this country may have a high incidence of juvenile delinquency, such behavior is also present in well established families where the children do not suffer from lack of money, social resources, and opportunity for education. Similarly, family disorganization is not limited to the socially deprived group that has been the traditional focus of social work concern. Separation, divorce, and extramarital relations are not uncommon in economically well-protected families. Although adolescents and young adults without educational advantages often have difficulty in establishing themselves vocationally and socially, college students also experience difficulty finding suitable employment and arriving at social goals that will make their efforts seem worth while.

When we consider the parents of today—whose lot it is to establish the goals and to live by the codes they would have their children emulate—we find attitudes and actions that bespeak their uncertainty about the roles they are attempting to carry, as well as their uncertainty about what values they want to instil in their children.[1]   Many parents, therefore, are transmitting to their children their own conflicts that stem from their feelings of isolation in their marriages, from their "unfinished business" with their primary families, and from their confusion about their parental role.   The results of their unhappiness and lack of fulfilment are to be found in the high number of persons who crowd the courts and mental health clinics.   In addition, there are the uncounted people who are prey to movements based on hostility and prejudice, as well as the vast number who suffer in silence, going about their business but, in the end, creating another generation of unhappy, conflicted parents.

Broadening the Base of Service

As social workers, we are at a crossroad, and the path we take will depend on our concept of the needs of families.   If we believe that the usual family should be able to meet and fulfil the psychological, social, emotional, biological growth needs of its members without additional social supports, we shall follow the traditional course of offering service to families with serious problems.   We shall choose another course, however, if we conclude, on the basis of current knowledge about family processes and about the influence of the socio-cultural setting on healthy life, that all families require additional supports and safeguards against the spread of social infection.   If we believe that the troubled family is a "thing apart," our focus will obviously be on pathology.   On the other hand, if we believe that the culture and social change contain the seeds for the development of difficulties in all families, we shall not be bound by a narrow psychological concern and deal only with families that have experienced actual impairment.   Rather, we shall be concerned with broad issues and endeavor to build immunity and resistance in all families to the germs of disturbances that are endemic in our society.   The need for preventive work by social institutions, particularly those that

[1] J. Milton Yinger, "The Changing Family in a Changing Society," *Social Casework*, Vol. XL, No. 8 (1959), p 419.

are committed to serving the family, is becoming increasingly clear. Family agencies, which have accumulated a vast fund of knowledge about family processes and the points of family vulnerability, are in a particularly strategic position to carry these new responsibilities.[2]

During the past twenty years family service agencies have undertaken a number of different approaches in the area of prevention. Their activities, quite naturally, have sprung directly from their treatment base. The initial effort took the form of an aggressive campaign to spread the knowledge that family counseling services were useful to people in all economic groups and social classes. An outgrowth of this experience was the development of a new self-image, as well as a new public image, of the family service agency. It came to be viewed not solely as a rescue service for families in a state of collapse, but also as a therapeutic service for families whose capacity for self-maintenance and self-direction was only partially impaired but whose well-being was threatened by incipient problems.

Although we were still preoccupied at this time with problem solving and with the correction of difficulties that had already been precipitated, these efforts were sowing a preventive seed. The concept of the value of early intervention when families encountered problems of individual adjustment or interpersonal relationships was widely interpreted to the community.[3]

The development of "family life education" programs was a next logical step. This preventive endeavor was stimulated by such factors as the increase in our technical knowledge, the development of wide-scale public health programs, and the popularity of adult education programs. In our agency, as well as others, caseworkers undertook to translate the principles derived from their experiences in therapy into concepts that could be presented and discussed in groups. Among the subjects of such

[2] Sanford N. Sherman, "A Forward Look at Family Service," presented at the Tenth Annual Meeting of Jewish Family Service Association of Newark, N. J., December 6, 1956.

[3] Ira M Younker, "Family Counseling in Action Today," *Social Casework*, Vol. XXIX, No. 3 (1948), p. 106. Frances T Levinson (Beatman), "Counseling in the Family Agency," *Proceedings of the National Conference of Jewish Social Work*, 1947.

sessions were the processes of parenting, marital adjustment, and intergenerational relations.

Of special significance in such organization of concepts was the development of indices of healthy family living and of symptoms of potential dangers. Although we were endeavoring to collate our subjective ideas about family roles, we unwittingly arrived at generalizations that in actual fact provided a framework to assess modes of conduct and means of adjustment. This framework made it possible for us to set up discussion groups for mothers, fathers, wives and husbands, and adolescent children—in short, for people of any age who have the capacity to learn through cognitive processes. These educational institutes, which might consist of several sessions, were made available to natural groups in places they normally frequent, such as community centers, schools, and religious institutions. Such an approach to "well families" was the logical next step in the preventive efforts of family agencies.[4] The fact that family life education became an important part of many agencies' programs was doubtless related to the emergence in the community of popular and useful programs of group education. Also the fact that family agencies had something helpful to say to people stimulated their leaders to develop such programs.[5] Social institutions in the community were also urging family agencies to assume a more authoritative role in the areas of their special knowledge.

A parallel development, and to some extent an offshoot of the family life education programs, has been the extended use of mass media—magazines, newspapers, books, radio, television, movies, and other art forms. Originally, family service agencies turned to these sources of public information for help in advising people about the existence of social agencies and the value of seeking professional help for family problems. Efforts were directed toward informing the public of the existence of family

4 Jerome D. Diamond, "Group Counseling in the Family Agency," *Social Casework,* Vol. XXXII, No. 5 (1951), p. 207; Gertude K. Pollak, "Family Life Education: Its Focus and Techniques," *Social Casework,* Vol. XXXIV, No. 5 (1953), p 198.
5 Committee on Family Life Education of the Family Service Association of America, "Family Life Education," *FSAA Highlights,* Vol. XII, No. 5 (1951), p. 65.

agencies and of the applicability of their helping principles to various family problems and to all groups in the community. One purpose was to help the public avoid the use of self-appointed and inadequately prepared "advice givers."

Since many individuals were hungry for guidance, reassurance, and authentic knowledge, they were creating a demand for concepts and precepts of sound family life. Their own unhappy experiences, as well as the anxieties evoked by the increasing spread of social problems, propelled them to look for authoritative sources of direction and reassurance. Conscientious writers for mass media turned to the family service agency for help in formulating content and in screening popularized versions of professional content. The readiness of agencies to move beyond their direct client contacts and to undertake educational programs led to their participation in efforts to popularize technical concepts. As a result, the public was enabled to make discriminations between lay and professional advice. Agencies undertook to work with representatives of mass media because they felt a responsibility to attempt to influence the value orientations of families in our communities, and to endeavor to intervene in the revision of values, a process which heretofore had been largely autonomous and unconscious. Although family agencies recognize their responsibility for making public, through the use of mass media, the knowledge they have distilled and accumulated about family processes and the transmission of appropriate values, they do not now consider this responsibility as solely theirs. They believe such efforts call for a partnership with other institutions and professions whose experience enables them to offer families the kind of knowledge that can prevent difficulties.

Each of these steps, which have added to the preventive role of family agencies, was hard won. Our previous efforts had been in the direction of deepening our diagnostic skill and treatment ability in order to be of help to families who were already hurt and in difficulty. Heavy demands for services, together with limited agency resources, tended to create considerable professional conflict about deflecting our energy and time away from treatment responsibilities, despite the mandate to ourselves to find avenues for using our knowledge preventively. Also, our natural caution about making information available, when we were not sure how it would be presented or used, added to our conflict. These uncertainties and concerns were inevitable during the process of moving from one stage to the next. Some good reasons, and many poor ones, were put forth by those who wished to maintain the status quo. Fortunately, there were some visionaries in the field who believed that a test of professional maturity was a willingness to risk experimenting with new ways of helping—of expanding the influence of the social work profession and thereby promoting sound family living in the whole community. As one of the leaders in this forward movement, Dr. Gomberg envisioned a profession that was characterized by an exacting demand for competent practice; a clear conceptual base; reciprocity with related disciplines with mutual enrichment of each; and a keen sense of responsibility for the common good.[6] He knew well that with professsional maturity comes the arduous task of spreading the word; and that with the rights of a profession to be heard go the responsibilities of using itself to its greatest capacity

Present Responsibilities for Preventive Services

The question before us today is whether the current preventive programs of family agencies, even with some expansion, constitute the most that they should offer, or whether they should place their preventive responsibility on a par with their treatment responsibility. If we favor the latter course, we must develop a field of preventive practice that has an identity and content of its own and a program whose purpose is to immunize families against social ills. In this dream of the future, the vision takes the form of a public family health program. Such a program would be based on the premise that the maintenance of family stability is a specific responsibility of society and that society has an obligation to develop appropriate means to achieve this end.

It seems to me that family agencies have a particular responsibility for initiating preventive programs and that they are now

[6] Sanford N. Sherman, Frances L. Beatman, and Nathan W. Ackerman, M.D., "Concepts of Family Striving and Family Distress. The Contribution of M. Robert Gomberg," *Social Casework*, Vol. XXXIX, No. 7 (1958), p. 383.

89

ready to implement this idea, which has often been put forth in the past but has never been put to the test. Such a program might be viewed as an adaptation of the "check-up" plan applied to mental health and social functioning. There are dental, medical, and other forms of check-up for the individual which have become part of our way of life. We rely on these programs to protect us, and to guide our activities along more healthful, energy-saving lines. The usefulness of an analogous form of check-up for family living would appear obvious.

The idea of check-up might be based on the familiar family life cycle. The nuclear family is founded, so to speak, when two individuals emerge from their families of origin, with separately forged psychosocial identities, and form a union. The family goes through developmental stages marked by changes in function and structure during its life cycle. Each phase or stage of development, beginning with the initial union of the marital couple, is accompanied by a crisis which must find some resolution in the continuing growth of the family organism. These developmental stages might be enumerated chronologically—courtship, marriage, the first pregnancy and birth, the first separation in nursery school, and so on.

Natural crises in family life tend to arise because of the conflicting and changing values in our culture and because of the instability and variability of our models of courtship, marriage, and parenting. Since the conflicts of individuals, as well as their interpersonal conflicts, are largely resolved unconsciously, they continue to be troublesome issues that may retard or fixate their growth. The crisis points in the life cycle are therefore natural points at which inventories of normal development might be made, in order to help the comparatively healthy family move along the pathway of normal adaptation and growth. The preventive idea is based on an assumption that help could be given to families at the sequential points of crisis and change in their lives. It would require a program that would provide, in a structuralized way, a professional assessment of the family's capacities and its processes of adaptation to these crisis points. It would also require a type of service that would buttress the healthy and flexible elements in a family and help dissipate unnecessary apprehensions.

90

The inventories would also serve as a method of "case finding," that is, the identification of families that might need some form of therapy.

Such a program would be designed to give a family an opportunity to review its questions with a family specialist who is equipped to make an appraisal of its operation as a family unit and of the functioning of its members in relation to each other and in the roles they carry outside the home. In addition to benefiting the family, such a program would contribute to the general welfare. It is generally recognized that intrafamilial processes hold the key to the individual's ability to function adequately and positively in his extrafamilial roles.

The various disciplines concerned with the family have been providing formulations and techniques that will help us understand the cross-sectional operation of the family and that will add to our clinical knowledge about individual functioning. The problem of identifying the diagnostically most significant intrafamilial, interpersonal processes requires continued research. Present increased understanding of the family unit, however, as well as our increased skill in working with the members as a group, have led us to an appreciation of the value of helping families as they move from one stage of family life to another.

In envisioning such a preventive program, we start with more questions than answers. In addition to the professional questions of what might be included in a significant inventory and how the inventory can be read so it gives an accurate picture, there are administrative questions related to structure, auspices, promotion, community education, financing, and all the other demons that stalk any new venture. But the major question is whether we are ready to venture this far from home base. In a field where learning can never be complete, we tend to wait for the comfort of final solutions and ultimate knowledge before we venture on new applications and programs. Our responsibility for study must be an ongoing one—but we have a responsibility to the community that must be carried concurrently. If we believe we have arrived at a point where our knowledge can be used in ways that will help families avoid difficulties, we have a responsibility for finding ways of making it available to the people who need it.

Medicine, too, had to decide at one time whether all of its resources should be directed toward treatment and cure or whether a part should be released for preventive efforts.

Social living today creates such widespread confusion that people have a great need for reassurance. Their uneasiness leads to many "fads" and people tend to follow advice too easily, often misplacing their confidence. We have the responsibility for developing and providing better ways for persons to deal with their confusions. A demand for professional help in this area can come only if the public knows that such services are available, that the use of them is socially acceptable, and that families themselves cannot be held responsible for "checking up" on their own processes. The general acceptance of public health programs of education and health maintenance, such as the well-baby clinics, provides a helpful base for the development of a "family health maintenance program."

The directives for establishing preventive services are many and they give family service agencies little choice about their obligations. Their historical role has been to protect and give service to families, applying the most advanced knowledge at their command.

Although the major function of the family service agency has been to provide direct service to troubled families, it has also carried responsibility for participating in efforts to improve the common welfare. By carrying both a treatment and a social planning role, the family agency has in a sense served as the chief social institution through which the theoretical contributions of many disciplines are sifted, synthesized, and integrated into a whole for the purpose of strengthening the family. Our responsibility is now to take our refined knowledge and find ways of making it available for "mass consumption." We have participated and will continue to participate in general programs that develop public understanding of mental health principles, alter educational concepts, and stand for the right of every human being to have appropriate help available in times of trouble.

The need is for a concept of responsibility and an appreciation of current knowledge of family dynamics which will make it possible to reach out to families and offer them a program designed to promote positive family life.

In planning for check-up services, we would probably find it advisable, structurally, to build them in at natural points of the family life cycle. For example, premarital consultation would be a "natural" for the planned parenthood clinic, and subsequent check-up service would be appropriate for prenatal clinics, nurseries, schools, health clinics, and so forth. The family service agency's responsibility would cut horizontally across such specialized resources. It seems likely that such specialized services will not be developed unless the family service agency, with its concern about the complete family life cycle, acts as prompter, initiator, tester, and standard setter.

Conclusion

In this discussion of a check-up program, we have been considering several different tasks any preventive service must fulfil. One is that of assessment or inventory-taking. As Nathan Ackerman has said, there are "islands of health and islands of distress" in the family. Whatever balance is struck depends on the family's capacity to meet, adapt, and grow through various stages of crisis and change. The second task is to buttress the healthy components in the family, providing reassurances about culturally-induced anxieties, making universal that which should be universal but is felt to be unique by an individual or family. The third task is to assume the concomitant responsibilities that go with a preventive program; individuals or families with problems and conflicts of pathological dimensions should be helped to recognize their need for therapy and motivated to use appropriate therapeutic resources.

We all know that establishing mass preventive programs would be a tremendous undertaking and would require untold effort and organization to influence public acceptance of them. The question facing family agencies is whether they have any choice but to move in this direction. Such a service may hold the key to helping a family function as a more balanced unit, able to meet the growth needs of its members. Any field of practice dedicated to the service of man must at times take an inventory of its accomplishments vis-à-vis its charge, and then decide on its future direction. Such decisions have been made by the fields of medicine and education, and it is becoming evident that a decision must now be made by those disciplines that have undertaken to understand the family and to meet the challenge of the family in our society. The enhancement of the welfare and the mental health of our society cannot be achieved by a laissez-faire attitude. It is the combination of continued internal professional responsibility and mass programs for dissemination of knowledge which will fill the gaps in the social control processes of today. This leaves to social workers and the related professions the responsibility for engaging in assertive—even adventurous—undertakings

The Study of Intrafamilial Alignments and Splits in Exploratory Family Therapy

Lyman C. Wynne

ALIGNMENTS AND SPLITS, alliance and alienation, are phenomena observable in all persisting groups, including families. The purpose of this paper is to focus explicitly upon alignments and splits as structural points of reference for the study of the various levels of family functioning during the course of family therapy. I suggest that this orientation may prove to be particularly valuable for persons engaged in the scrutiny of the social system aspects of families seen in a therapeutic setting. A shift to thinking of families in terms of dynamic wholes or social systems (more accurately, *sub*systems) is an approach repetitiously recommended but difficult to achieve. The focus upon alignments and splits within family systems indicates an effort in that direction, hopefully of such kind that personality functioning will remain in view and may even be illuminated.

Many family researchers, including our own group at the National Institute of Mental Health, have used the concept of role in describing structure and conflict within family systems.[1] Although the role concept has been valuable in the analysis of

---

[1] See, for example, Nathan W Ackerman, *The Psychodynamics of Family Life*, Basic Books, New York, 1958, Irving Ryckoff, Juliana Day, and Lyman C Wynne, "Maintenance of Stereotyped Roles in the Families of Schizophrenics," *AMA Archives of Psychiatry*, Vol. I, No. 1, (1959), pp. 93–98; John P Spiegel, "The Resolution of Role Conflict Within the Family," *Psychiatry*, Vol. XX, No 1, (1957), pp. 1–16; Lyman C. Wynne, Irving M Ryckoff, Juliana Day, and Stanley I. Hirsch, "Pseudo-Mutuality in the Family Relationships of Schizophrenics," *Psychiatry*, Vol. XXI, No. 2, (1958), pp 205–220.

long-range, over-all features of family life, it appears to be un-wieldy as an aid in describing detailed therapeutic shifts and sequences. Communications-analysis of discrete messages,[2] on the other hand, although useful in the study of fine details of thera-peutic transactions, does not readily lend itself to descriptions of organizational or structural features of the family as a whole. I am proposing a focus upon alignments and splits in family therapy as a supplement to these other kinds of orientation, which we and other investigators will continue to use for various purposes. Presumably no single manner of formulation or study is equally suitable for all the diverse research and therapeutic problems now being examined in the family setting.

Definitions and Principles

What, more specifically, do I mean by alignment or alliance and split or alienation? An alignment can be defined as the percep-tion or experience of two or more persons that they are joined together in a common endeavor, interest, attitude, or set of values, and that in this sector of their experience they have positive feel-ings toward one another. A split is here defined as a comparable perception or experience of opposition, difference, or estrange-ment, with associated negative feelings. The alignments and splits within a social system define, to a considerable extent, the emotional organization of the system.

It is obvious that alignments, with the positive emotional ties they entail, are one of the features of family life, or of any social system, that help establish the nature of its organization. But it is no less true that splits, however negatively toned, also shape and sustain the structure of social systems. Both alignments and splits are functional in the homeostatic maintenance of families as social systems. Within an actively functioning family social organization the splits cannot be given up any more easily than the alignments.

[2] For example, Gregory Bateson, Don D. Jackson, Jay Haley, and John H. Weakland, "Toward a Theory of Schizophrenia," *Behavioral Science*, Vol. I, No. 4, (1956), pp. 251–264; John H. Weakland and Don D. Jackson, "Patient and Therapist Observations on the Circumstances of a Schizophrenic Episode," *A.M.A. Archives of Neurology and Psychiatry*, Vol. LXXIX, No. 4, (1958), pp. 554–574.

Alignments and splits may, of course, exist on several levels of consciousness and with a variety of content. For example, an outburst of bickering and manifest contempt between two persons represents on one level an obvious splitting in their relation. While observing the context and timing of such events in family therapy, we have been impressed by the regularity with which bickering, for example, occurs just after signs of unacknowledged fondness or alliance have appeared, either between the same two persons or between one of them and a third person. Such sequences often form the core of some of the most characteristic transactions in family therapy. They are not, of course, unique to family therapy, but the study of such sequences over a period of time, as the therapeutic process unfolds, will help reveal how the various levels of functioning in the family system are dynamically linked and experientially separated or dissociated.

Stated in a highly schematic way, the approach I suggest for starting to unravel the interpersonal structure of family therapy groups is simply this: When an alignment has developed within a given family therapy group, look for an emerging split at another level or in another part of the group; if a split emerges, expect an associated alignment to come into view. By shifting one's focus, sequentially, from alignment to split and back again, one may, I suggest, become progressively more intimately acquainted with the structure and dynamics of the therapy group as a social subsystem.

In terms of generalized theory, this approach is an application of the principle of dynamic equilibrium: a change (in this case, an emerging alignment or split) in any part of a system whose components are interdependent reverberates to produce change in other parts of the system.

A Case Illustration

My interest in alignments and splits in family therapy groups began with the observation of transactions such as the following:

> A father opens a family therapy session by directing a series of queries to his recently hospitalized 25-year-old son about his ward life: "How they feed you over here? . . . Can you sleep all right? . . . Who'd you play chess with? . . . Anybody

97

your age here? . . . Do they have picture shows here?" The son responds to each question in pedantically elaborated "factual" detail. Meanwhile, the mother is busy smoothing scarcely visible wrinkles in her dress; the therapist adjusts and readjusts the position of his footstool. With increasing satisfaction, the father comments on his son's replies with statements such as: "Well, you don't have to be over here forever. . . . Don't feel as relaxed as you do at home, huh? . . . The chess players here can't be very accomplished. . . . Well, anyway, you can almost look out the window here and see your home."

As the father is laughing with pleasure over this last comment, the mother speaks quietly to the son, "I have some things out in the car for you, two boxes and a pair of slacks. . . . A box of—"

The father brusquely interrupts, "Well, let's get started here, so don't bring it up now." He turns to the therapist, "I'm in your hands. I want to be whatever you want me to be."

Certain structural features of the family and the family therapy group are apparent even in this brief fragment of a session. The son's move from home to hospital ward has clearly been experienced by the father as a potential, if but temporary, loosening (incipient split) in his relation with his son. The father undercuts the new ward alignments of his son and at the same time endeavors to establish continuity in the relation with him. The mother, who meanwhile has appeared self-absorbed, finally attempts to displace the father with her own effort at alignment with the son, but this is promptly disrupted by the father. (Later, in the work with this family, it became apparent that the mother's patience rested upon her faith in a covert and enduring alignment with the son which would flourish more openly some day when the father would be safely dead.)

The therapist has been biding his time in this particular early session while noting to himself certain disquieting feelings of being excluded (split off) from the family scene. The first statement addressed to the therapist in this session comes only after the overt family structure has been re-established, after the emerging alignments of the son with outsiders and with his mother are again out of view. The split between the parents is quickly sealed off when the father turns to the therapist. His statement to the therapist might overtly seem to bridge the implicit, widening gap between therapist and family. However, the most immediate experience of the therapist is perplexity: How can one engage solidly with the father while he professes such complete malleability? The alignment which the father says he wishes to make with the therapist would obviously be on a superficial level and would screen from view any potential opposition between the father and therapist. In addition, the alignment which the father offers the therapist would be on an all-absorbing basis that would tend to leave out the mother and son and thus split them off from the therapist. For the therapist to accept at face value the father's offer of "co-operation" would leave the therapist entangled in one part of the family's network of alignments and splits, but cut off from opportunities to explore and understand other, concealed parts of the network.

Perhaps this example may suggest how attention to the shifting patterns of alignment and split in family therapy groups may give clues not only to various levels of the family structure and connections between them, but also to maneuvers used by the participants in maintaining, changing, or restoring the structure. Pitfalls for the therapist, as well as opportunities for exploratory clarification, may also be apparent in this example.

Characteristics of Exploratory Family Therapy

Because these observations derive from "family therapy," which is by no means a standardized procedure, I shall now turn to a description of the kind of family therapy in which I have been participant. I shall also convey my current impressions, highly tentative, of conditions for family therapy that may facilitate our understanding of the underlying structure and dynamics of family units. My comments are based upon experience with family therapy used as both a research and a therapeutic technique in the Family Studies program at the National Institute of Mental Health.[8] In this program some thirty families have been seen in

[8] Recent participants in the family therapy of this program have been in addition to myself, Dr. Juliana Day, Stanley Hirsch, Dr. Thomas Lewis, Dr. C. Peter Rosenbaum, and Dr. Leslie Schaffer, and, as consultants, Dr. Irving C. Ryckoff and Dr. Harold Searles.

family therapy two or three hours weekly for periods from six weeks to three years. The families have generally been composed of two parents and two or more offspring, including a hospitalized, psychiatrically ill, late adolescent or young adult.

First, our goals in this program have been primarily exploratory; our focal concern has been the understanding and clarification of the nature and sources of the tensions and difficulties of the family and of the family therapy group. Such a goal involves a kind of family therapy different from what might be called family counseling, in which the primary intent of the therapist is the more direct relief of anxiety and symptoms, for example, by making suggestions about altered ways in which the family members might deal with each other. In exploratory family therapy, the therapist expects that symptoms and tensions may increase as obscure and masked family patterns come to light, but he believes that maximal long-range therapeutic gain, together with greater research understanding, may result from continuing to focus upon the nature of the family patterns rather than upon immediate symptom relief.

Exploratory family therapy also should be distinguished from family sessions which are primarily intended to facilitate concomitant individual psychotherapy. The distinctive principles and problems of "exploratory" family therapy, as I am using the term here, rest upon the assumption that the "patient," the subject of the family therapy, is not an individual or an aggregate of individuals meeting to talk about an individual, but is the interlocking *system* of family relationships.

Exploratory family therapy may follow, accompany, or lead to individual psychotherapy or psychoanalysis with one or more of the family members. However, during the family therapy sessions themselves the orientation is not primarily toward the individual personality but to the relationships within the family. Moreover, the therapist need not, indeed had better not, embark upon family therapy with a preconceived goal either that this family should remain together as a social system or that the family members should disband and go their separate ways as quickly as possible. In contrast, exploratory family therapy may lead to clearer perception of the difficulties involved in making

100

any lasting change. Such clarification may help free the family from shared maneuvers which thwart genuine choice of direction.

In the Family Studies program at the National Institute of Mental Health, a routine procedure has evolved for engaging families in exploratory therapy. After a preliminary screening session or two with the entire family, we usually devote approximately six weeks to diagnostic evaluation and study of treatment potentialities in each family. During this period conjoint family therapy sessions are held twice weekly; a home visit, psychological testing, and history-taking interviews also take place. Two purposes are served by beginning with a clearly defined evaluation period. First, we identify and select for further family therapy those family members who are participants in the currently active and emotionally meaningful organization (social system) of family relationships. Second, we try to ascertain whether these family members and therapists have the capacity to contain their participation, without disruptive acting out, within definable limits necessary in any effective treatment program.

The task of discovering which family members should be included in the family therapy group is not so simple as it may initially seem. Certain family members may be reluctant to come to evaluation sessions, may claim to be psychologically remote from family problems, and yet later will actively disrupt the family therapy if they have not been included in the therapy group. On the other hand, if the therapists insist that all biologically related family members take part even though they no longer have their main emotional ties with each other, if their past together has been displaced by marital or new familial ties, the treatment will lack immediacy and is likely to drift unproductively. Other persons may not be biologically related to the family, yet fulfil significant family roles. In one instance, early in our experience with family therapy, we excluded such a person from the family sessions despite his wish and the family's agreement that he come; later, he aligned with two offspring, split them off from the therapy group, and sabotaged the work with this family.

Intentional variations in the therapy-group composition may help evaluate, as part of "family diagnosis," who should be included in the family therapy on a longer-term basis However, once the evaluation is over and a decision to proceed with exploratory family therapy has been reached, a high degree of stability in the group's composition is essential if the underlying structure and conflicts of this particular group are to be deeply explored and brought into verbal expression.

In our work we have observed that the absence of any participant from a particular session is experienced both by that person and the rest of the group as a splitting-off or alienation. If such absences occur only occasionally, it may be possible to explore their meaning in the subsequent sessions and to clarify the characteristics of the alienation. However, excessively frequent or haphazard changes in the group composition may make it impossible to explore the meanings of any particular change before another absence again splits the group. One may then find that the "natural unfolding" of the deeper levels of functioning of the group cannot develop.

Absence of any participant from a therapy session should be regarded as his acting out a split within the group As in all forms of psychotherapy, acting out is of course disruptive. Acting out in family therapy, however, may disrupt not only the therapy but also long-standing, complex family ties and hence is even more intensely disturbing than in other forms of therapy. We have observed that in nearly all families—not just in families of delinquents—family members fear that speaking one's mind will result in physical assault, uncontrollable intimacy, or abrupt separations. The family therapy setting, like all therapy settings, must provide a safe place for free communication as a basic condition for effective treatment. Insistence by the therapists upon stability in the group composition helps greatly in weathering storms of anxiety or psychosis and in conveying the therapist's confidence that such disturbance can be converted into verbal communication.

Acting out *between sessions*, however, poses problems that have different dimensions in family therapy than in other forms of psychotherapy. The potentialities for acting out between sessions among the family members, if not between the family members and the therapist, are greater than in conventional group

therapy, where the members ordinarily do not see each other between sessions. In our program, usually at least one family member is in the hospital; this has provided some additional safeguards
against acting out between sessions. We have been surprised,
however, to find that once the family members experience the
sessions as "different" and as a safe place in which to communicate,
even highly disturbed families are able to "hold over" strong
feelings from one session to the next.

As I have implied, exploratory family therapy requires particular characteristics in the therapist as well as in the family. It seems
essential that the therapist be active and aggressive enough to define and insist upon the minimal conditions and limits within
which the participants can eventually take the risks of free communication. In addition, the family therapist should have a
genuine orientation to the family as a whole, as a social system, so
that even when he temporarily becomes absorbed in a personal
way with an individual family member, he is able to return to
a family-wide perspective. Such a "balanced" orientation is difficult to maintain, especially when the whole family has an invest-
ment in perceiving all its difficulties as located in the presenting
patient.

Therapists tend to perceive the family's difficulties as located
in the parents. Usually such a view of the family constitutes a
split with the parents and an alignment, in the form of over-
identification, with the presenting patient. When only the presenting patient is in therapy, without family therapy, the alienation of the therapist from the rest of the family may remain latent
for a long time, especially if the therapy is cloistered in a hospital.
Eventually, however, as all hospital psychotherapists know, such
covert splits are apt to reach explosive proportions and lead to
precipitous disruption of treatment. In family therapy such
patterns are more difficult to ignore in their early stages. Without
adequate limit-setting and interpretation, therapist-family splits
will bring the treatment to a premature halt. However, the
stimulus and opportunity for therapeutic intervention at an early
and manageable stage in the development of such splits are obviously greatly heightened by the face-to-face encounter with the
family.

103

We have found that supplementary observational techniques may assist family therapists in keeping in mind parts of the family system that they may otherwise persistently overlook. Tape recordings played back for discussion and the use of one-way observation mirrors with subsequent discussion between therapists and observers have been especially valuable supplementary techniques in our program.

In observing family therapy, we have found it especially rewarding to note what is going on with the silent members of the group, while changes—either alignments or splits—are appearing elsewhere in the therapy group.[4] Nonverbal clues to the participation of the silent ones in the shifting group pattern then regularly become apparent: a sudden scowl or a quick, warm glance at another group member; a new-found interest in one's fingernails; a shift in the seating arrangement, and so on.

Another valuable source of data about incipient alignments and splits is the subjective experience of the therapists, their shifting feelings and fantasies in relation to the other members of the family therapy group. Often the first clues of unconscious levels of alliance and alienation within the group lie in the therapist's awareness of his own subjective experience. For example, a therapist may note in himself at a particular time some unexpectedly warm feelings toward one of the family members. If he can regard these feelings as a form of data about an incipient, although unexpressed, alignment between himself and the family member, he may then reflect upon the timing and context of the appearance of these feelings and recognize evidence of an otherwise unnoticed associated shift in the therapy-group structure; for example, he may note a subtle belittling and alienating quality in the ostensibly "constructive" suggestions of a second family member toward both himself and the family member with whom he felt aligned.

Alignments and Splits in a Schizophrenic Family

I shall illustrate some of the problems involving alignments and splits in family therapy as they appeared in a particular family that included an overtly schizophrenic offspring.

[4] Dr. Thomas Main, of Cassel Hospital, England, has particularly called our attention to the usefulness of systematically observing the silent participants. (personal communication)

Mr. Little, aged 50, came from a poverty-stricken southern rural background, had a grade-school education, and was now employed as a filing clerk at a rather low salary. Mrs. L, aged 47, with high school education, had been employed most of her adult life as a secretary, at a higher salary than her husband. Susan, a student, was 15 years old at the time therapy began. Betty, an 18-year-old daughter, had become overtly schizophrenic two months before her high school graduation, and three months before admission to our program. Her illness was characterized by apathetic withdrawal to the home, bizarrely obsessional concern about cleanliness and being a "good girl," disorganized paranoid thinking, and finally, a catatonic state of such severity that she had not eaten voluntarily for two weeks and had developed marked ankle edema due to her fixed position.

The therapists for this particular family were Dr. Peter Rosenbaum, who also became the hospitalized patient's individual therapist, and myself. Our first direct contact with any members of this family was in a pre-admission family session. It is of interest to note the presenting features of this initial session, since they provide clues to the alignments and splits of the family at the beginning of therapy.

After one of the therapists inquired why they were here, Mr. L hesitantly took the lead by saying softly that they wanted the therapists to help their daughter Betty. He suggested that the therapists ask Betty what her problems were. Betty, in a deeply catatonic state, was unresponsive. After a silence, one of the therapists expressed the hope that Betty would feel free to speak if she wished, but since she did not take up their suggestion, he invited the parents to go ahead and tell something of what they had noticed. The mother began, but the father interrupted, now in a louder and more assured voice than previously. "She started," he said, "with a-crying spells. . . . She seemed as though it was something bothering her and seemed as though we can't find out what it is. . . . She'd just act like she had lost her best friend, you see. And I try to find out. I went around and talked to school teachers and principal. One teacher said that she was a little angel. I patted him on the back. I said, 'Keep your good work up.' I knew that Betty was a good girl. I do know she's a good disposition. Good girl."

Thus, the initial minutes with this family indicated that currently Betty was silently estranged from the rest of the family and that the father was most actively involved in repairing his loosening bond with Betty by using outside intermediaries to agree that she was a "good girl." During this session he expressed doubt about his own capacity to reach her directly. We learned that he had also consulted, in addition to us, a long series of other doctors, several clergymen, and several government officials. In his effort at re-alignment with Betty, he did not join with his wife on any point, either in the session or in his description of the past. Indeed, he actively interrupted her and shut her out from expressing her views.

Two closely linked features seemed prominent in the structure of the L family—an alignment between the father and the compliant, "angelic" side of Betty, and a split between the parents. The following excerpts from early family therapy sessions may serve to convey the quality of these two presenting features of the family, and the close connection between them:

> *Betty:* You can spend all day long cleaning the house. . . .
> *Susan:* You're not supposed to.
> *Betty:* You're not supposed to, but you can. It's not hard to do.
> *Father:* Yes, I agree with you, Betty, you can. You can spend all day in there. Especially my house. It needs a good cleaning.
> *Susan:* It does not. Any house uh. . . .
> *Father:* I will say, she's smart. I think she kept that house fine.
> *Mother:* Nobody could suit you.
> *Father:* There's not a lazy bone in that girl.
> *Mother:* Yeah, but didn't we tell her though that we didn't want her to do that?
> *Father:* Somebody give her a . . . give her a chance, she'll be somewhere someday. She never refused to do anything I ask her. And she studied. Was only a couple a months ago when she started cleaning like this, but . . . but she always was smart, even when she was a little thing. . . . She's always never refused to do anything.

On another occasion, Mr. L, speaking of his wife:

> *Father:* So as I say, you can't trust her to lock a door, you can't. . . .
> *Mother:* That's what *you* say.
> *Father:* If she . . . there were a thing you'd tell her to do, she'll do object. That's all . . . that—that'll answer the whole question. Susan'll tell you, Betty'll tell you. Everything you tell her to do *right*, she'll deliberately do it *opposite* from what you

106

tell her . . . to cause trouble. Then she'll argue with you. She'll put up an argument.

Mother: I don't argue. I wish I knew. . . .

Father: And cause the whole house an uproar. So that's the story. . . .

Mother: Just because you think things are right, it's not saying they're so. . . . Just like Betty's friends. You found something wrong with every one of them. Every one she ever had was something wrong. Just because they went to a particular church or something. My sister, she run around with a married man. My brother, he was no good, to you.

When the split between the father and Betty, on one side, and the mother and, often, Susan, on the other, was most heated, the father would redouble his expressions of affection and admiration for Betty.

On several such occasions he then moved to sit next to Betty and reached over to touch her arm. An underlying split between father and Betty now abruptly became explicit. Betty pulled her arm away and almost jumped to the other side of the room. Instead of reacting directly to Betty, the father at such points usually launched into an attack upon the mother—the mother had a vicious temper and did not talk "sweet and gentle like a mother should." The mother characteristically replied with a flat denial that sealed off the split from further exploration, saying, "Well, that's all right." On some occasions the mother would then turn to the therapists, ostensibly aligning herself with them by asking a general question, such as "If a mother goes to the PTA and takes her daughter to the Girl Scouts and church groups, how could the daughter later get sick?" Susan would then often split with her mother, turn on her mother with a viciously toned, "Oh, you don't know nothin'." If the therapists tried to call a halt to explore any one of these leads or to comment on the sequences of the transactions, Betty might say chidingly to the therapist, "If you try to do *right*, you don't have to worry." While the therapist was catching his breath, she might add, "I will be glad to do anything you tell me to do," and then, staring off into space, "I think somebody may have done something to my body." The father would take such a statement as a signal for re-alignment with Betty and would earnestly plead with her to tell him if she meant the boy she had

107

met at a church camp two years ago. The mother, however, would interrupt to correct the name of the boy mentioned by the father.

Being extraordinarily intuitive individuals, the therapists sensed a certain chaos in such proceedings—highly stereotyped chaos! They began to have the uneasy suspicion that they were learning firsthand how one might learn to be schizophrenic. In the families of schizophrenics the structure of alignments and splits seems to shift in a bewilderingly rapid fashion, but with one feature of great constancy: the meaning of any *particular* alignment or split does not clearly emerge. Particular meanings on the one hand are kept amorphous and not fully discriminable, or, on the other hand, are psychologically split off, dissociated, or fragmented, kept separate in a kind of psychological *apartheid* from the context of the other alignments and splits that might otherwise lend coherent meaning to any particular relationship or transaction.

It is pointed out in a recent paper by Dr. Leslie Schaffer and others of our staff [5] that one of the ways in which therapists characteristically behave under chaotic circumstances of this sort is to deny their own experience and that of the family by rushing precipitously to find an underlying pattern and meaning in the proceedings. This is called "making an interpretation." Actually, the family members, too, try to rescue themselves from the devastating impact of chaotic experience by making their own brand of interpretations.

Pseudo-Mutuality and Pseudo-Hostility

The self-rescuing operations used under such conditions by families—and sometimes by therapists—can be loosely classified under two main headings. We have previously described the first operation, labeling it pseudo-mutuality.[6] Pseudo-mutuality is a type of surface alignment that blurs and obscures from recognition and conscious experience both underlying splits and diver-

[5] Leslie Schaffer, Lyman C. Wynne, Juliana Day, and Alexander Halperin, "On the Nature and Sources of the Psychiatrist's Experience with the Family of the Schizophrenic," to be published in *Psychiatry*, August or November, 1961.
[6] Wynne *et al.*, "Pseudo-Mutuality in the Family Relations of Schizophrenics." *Op. cit.*

gences, on the one hand, and deeper affection and alignment, on the other hand. Pseudo-mutuality involves a level of experience in which underlying unsettled business is "settled" or fixed by a kind of alignment that forestalls further exploration of the relationship. The implicit threats of both greater divergence and greater intimacy remain undiscriminated and undifferentiated (amorphously underdeveloped) or are, secondarily, defensively blurred.

In the history of this particular family perhaps the most massive pseudo-mutuality had been that between the father and Betty prior to her open psychosis When Betty was most disturbed symptomatically, she actively attacked her father and strenuously, though psychotically, objected to their past relationship. Her objections became more articulate when she was at the same time in warm, good-humored alignment with either her sister or her individual therapist. Usually, however, initial, articulate objections quickly lapsed into ambiguities and then into obscure agreement with her father. On one occasion when the father touched Betty on the arm, Betty first drew away and then said, still quite forthrightly, "Petting between teenagers sometimes gets out of hand." The father replied, "A father's love is a father's love, a wife's love is a wife's love, and a daughter's love is a daughter's love, and that settles the problem." The two of them then went on to talk simultaneosuly in a kind of classic pseudo-mutuality, neither listening to the other but both periodically saying how fully they agreed with the other.

Betty would be particularly likely to embark upon such pseudo-mutual conversations if someone else, mother or therapist, had questioned the quality of the "harmony" between the father and herself. On one occasion, when the father had been haranguing Betty to sit down for her "own good," the therapist, noting the father's uneasiness when Betty was standing, wondered if the father also wanted her to sit down in order to make himself more comfortable. Betty interrupted the exploration of this question:

> *Betty:* He's trying to do to other people just what you're trying to do for your own self and other people. Constitutionalism. Written in the ... in the land just for one person. It's written by the people, for the people, and of the people.

109

Father: That's true, yeah.

Betty: In the United States. States what you get, united.

Father: That's why I say when she's sitting down, she's for the people, by the people.

Therapist: I gather that whatever Betty said you would get it turned into something that you would agree with?

Father: Well, she said it right! More than one person involved, more than one person. You must try to understand people when you're talkin' with 'em and talkin' to them. For instance, my wife, over there. I can't understand her. There's some people in the world that got a deeper thought, a deeper mind than others, can see further ahead than others. Well maybe Betty is just too smart for the average person. Maybe she can see further ahead than the average person can. What she said about the Constitution. She's deep. And I love to talk to a deep person.

Although the pseudo-mutuality in this family seemed to be primarily between the father and Betty, there were indications that the thinking of the other family members unconsciously went along with, or even covertly supported, the pattern. Although the mother complained about the father-Betty alignment, she stoutly insisted that she was helpless to do anything except complain. And, when Betty and her father were not *too* closely aligned, she maintained that a father and daughter *should* be fond of each other, just as she had been close to her own father. Speaking of Betty and Mr. L, she once said, "Her husband, I mean, my husband. . . ."

A second type of mechanism used most vividly and characteristically in the families of schizophrenics—though, once again, not *limited* to such families—can be called pseudo-hostility. Pseudo-hostility is a split or alienation, which may be exceedingly noisy and intense but remains limited to a surface level of experience and interaction. In a fixed and expectable way pseudo-hostility serves to blur and obscure the impact, on the one hand, of anxiety-producing intimacy and affection, and, on the other hand, of deepening hostility unfolding to destruction, acknowledged hopelessness, and lasting separation. Despite the difference in the surface content they present, pseudo-mutuality and pseudo-hostility are dynamically very similar. They both help maintain vulnerable relationships in a fixed form which somehow contains frightening wishes and impulses, but in which the positive aspects of these feelings and urges can make only a distorted contribution to the growth of the relationships and of the individuals who are involved.[7]

In the family therapy sessions, the parents in the L family launched into vitriolic attacks on each other in a highly sterotyped way; they said such fights had taken place throughout the twenty years of their marriage.[8] If splits of such duration and intensity represent *only* what they seem on the surface to be, it is likely that the marriage in which they occur would long since have been dissolved. Instead, they seem to bind the family together. Hurts of years ago are brought forth for display like treasured photographs from the family scrapbook.

Gradually we were able to gather clues about the many underlying functions which the marital split seemed to serve in the L family. We noticed that the parental fighting often began abruptly and intensely immediately after one daughter, usually Betty, had rebuffed or split with one of the parents. Eventually, we learned something of the enormous despair any sort of alienation or rebuff from the daughters brought to each parent. Their whole sense of worthwhileness as human beings seemed undermined if any element of real alienation from the daughters began to emerge. However, such despair rarely, especially in the early months of therapy, reached their awareness so long as they could plunge headlong into attacks and recriminations against each other.

The power of the daughters, particularly Betty, to nourish the marital split was enormous. Even a hint from Betty that she might

[7] The concept of pseudo-hostility is newly labeled in this paper. However, this idea was implied in the earlier paper on pseudo-mutuality when it was stated that the pseudo-mutual part of a family social system "may be very sharply split off from other parts of the family organization. . . . The splitting off of these persons or roles that are not involved in the pseudo-mutuality may . . . be highly functional for the family organization as a whole, even though these persons or roles may be consciously depreciated or ostracized." Wynne *et al., op. ott.*

[8] Lidz *et al.* classify the marital difficulties of the parents of schizophrenics under the headings of marital schism and marital skew. I agree that the marital patterns may differ from one family to the next and I do not wish to imply generalizations about all families of schizophrenics from this single example. The concepts of pseudo-mutuality and pseudo-hostility may apply, obviously, to any of the relations within a family, not just the marital relation. See Theodore Lidz, Alice R. Cornelison, Stephen Fleck, and Dorothy Terry, "The Intrafamilial Environment of Schizophrenic Patients: II. Marital Schism and Marital Skew," *American Journal of Psychiatry*, Vol. CXIV, No. 3 (1957), pp. 241–248.

reject one or the other of them would plunge the parents into renewed bickering, each attacking the other as a destructive parent and defending himself or herself as the essence of parental devotion and virtue. As her parents quarreled, Betty characteristically sat back in a haughty, rather queenly fashion, sometimes laughing uproariously, but not saying anything unless the parents seemed momentarily on the verge of bridging their differences. Thereupon, she would interject a reprimand toward one parent or the other, always, however, so ambiguously phrased that opposing conclusions could be drawn by the parents, and the marital quarrel would again flare up.

Again and again, when observing such sequences in family therapy, we have been impressed with the oversimplification contained in the idea that the schizophrenic child is the "victim" of "schizophrenogenic" parents. Rather, all family members, offspring and parents, are caught up in reciprocal victimizing—and rescuing—processes in which they are all tragically enmeshed.

On one occasion, when the father had been begging Betty for comfort and reassurance, he thoughtfully and sadly reflected in an unusual pause, "I feel like a li'l child toward my daughter." There was, indeed, evidence to suggest that both parents longed to return to the kind of relation each had had as a child in his own family of origin. Each had been consciously attracted to the other because each saw the filial devotion of the other; each had consciously hoped that the other would therefore be a devoted spouse. But feared complications, particularly sex, intruded into the marital relation and disrupted the underlying yearnings for tender care and affection. The father turned to his first daughter in a pseudomutual relation in which sexual and other complications could long be concealed. Later, when Betty matured physically (in a round, voluptuous fashion never achieved by her angular, ascetic mother), sexual problems became more difficult to manage.

After about two years of family therapy, an intense storm blew up when an effort was made by a therapist to differentiate out the sexual component in the relation between Betty and her father. The father experienced this move by the therapist as threatening total disruption of his relation with Betty, and for him this was equivalent to destroying or fragmenting him. ("Betty is not next to my heart; she is *part* of my heart.") Probably neither the father nor Betty could tolerate an open, clearly recognizable split with the other unless a new alignment with someone else, or with each other on another level, seemed available. Perhaps Betty was not quite so deeply threatened as her father was by this episode because she had a more solidly established alignment with someone else (her individual therapist).

The complicated problems in the therapy with this family, particularly with respect to the timing and groundwork necessary for interventions which have the effect of producing new alignments or splits, deserve the extensive consideration of an entire paper. Here I wish only to note that the marital split heightened the needs of both parents for new or altered alignments. The mother saw her own relation with both daughters in terms of physical care, particularly supplying food. She felt, however, that Betty, like the father, had always been less accepting of her cooking than Susan. In the father's eyes, the mother actively drove Betty out of the kitchen, and one of Betty's initial overt symptoms was a belief that the food prepared by the mother was poisoned. Although the mother had a limited alignment with the daughters, especially Susan, she also turned back to her own mother who lived nearby. Mrs. L had insisted that they live with her mother while the children were small, and in interviews she repeatedly mentioned how much she treasured her relations with her parents, brother, and sister. We also learned that during most of her marriage she had maintained an emotionally significant relation with her employer, who seemed to value greatly her secretarial skills. Mr. L, of course, bitterly attacked both her family of origin and her employer.

Concluding and Summary Comments

Although alignments and splits have their functional place in the organization of any family, it is our impression that their quality in normal families does differ from that of families that are psychiatrically disturbed but not primarily in a schizophrenic fashion. However, our work with some twenty families of schizophrenics and ten families of nonschizophrenic psychiatric patients has convinced us that there are significant differences—differences of degree rather than kind—between these two varieties of families. Within the families of nonschizophrenics there are of course extensive conflicts and defensive operations, but not, we believe, involving the same degree of amorphousness and fragmentation, or the same intense reliance on pseudo-mutual and pseudo-hostile mechanisms that disguise but help perpetuate the underlying problems. The detailed delineation of the differences between schizophrenic and nonschizophrenic families is a major task of our continuing research program.

I have attempted to suggest that a focus upon alignments and splits in a family therapy setting may help elucidate both the richness and the tangled, many-layered webs of family life. An orientation to alignments and splits, however, should not be regarded as an all-inclusive approach or as a replacement for other approaches to the study of family dynamics and structure. We believe it illuminates certain aspects of family life in an incisive, although perhaps an oversimplified, way. The approach relies upon a specific basic proposition. New or heightened alignments of two or more persons are regularly associated with some degree of alienation, or splitting off, from others within a same social organization; the converse is also true. Such splitting or alignment develops automatically and often with only subliminal registration of the previous change that induced it.

If an alignment (or split) is consciously perceived, it is possible that the subsequent alienation (or alignment) may be manifest chiefly in the subjective fantasies and associations of the person who is split off. If the person does not become aware of the change, he is more likely to respond in one of three other ways: (1) make active efforts to split or disrupt the alignment to which he is an outsider and sometimes to ally himself with one of the persons of the disrupted alignment; (2) seek a parallel, new alignment with another group member who is also outside the alignment; or (3) withdraw and reduce his integration with that group, either (a) by pursuing interests and alignments outside the group altogether, or (b) by becoming autistic, often in some sort of fantasied alignment that may replicate an earlier or childhood relationship.

114

Perhaps my illustrations may have suggested the possibility of conceptualizing a relation between the fragmentation and blurred amorphousness of schizophrenic family structure and similar features in the individual schizophrenic's personality structure. However, discussion of this question must be reserved for another occasion. Rather, I have tried here to describe one kind of setting, exploratory conjoint family therapy, in which family organization and maneuvers may be studied in terms of alignments and splits and through which therapeutic benefits may be derived.

The Biosocial Integration of Behavior in the Schizophrenic Family

Gregory Bateson

As a RESULT OF the growth of cybernetics especially and systems theory in general, we can now guess what the words "biosocial integration" denote but we are still very far from being able to say how any given biosocial system is integrated. We are at the stage where no particular theory can be proposed, although we know enough about what such theories should look like to be able to ask many questions.[1]

I shall assume that the words "biosocial integration" suggest that we look at biosocial systems—individual organisms, families, communities, or ecological systems—as entities that maintain stability by some combination of two processes: calibration and feedback.[2] And, in those cases that fail to maintain stability, I shall assume that we have to look for the pathologies that may be expected in these two processes or in their combination.

Feedback and Calibration

I shall first describe the processes separately. Feedback, which today is the more familiar term, is applied to a system containing

[1] The ideas in this paper emerge from research projects for the study of Schizophrenic Communication, financed by the Foundations' Fund for Research in Psychiatry administered by Stanford University and by Grant No. OM-324 from the National Institute of Mental Health administered by the Palo Alto Medical Research Foundation. These projects are a part of the research program of the Veterans Administration Hospital, Palo Alto, California.

[2] Horst Mittelstaedt, "Regelung in der Biologie," *Regelungstechnik*, Vol. II, No. 8 (1954), pp. 177–181.

a sense organ (such as the thermometer in the thermostatic control of a househeating system) that collects information about the value of some variable within the system. This information (that is, some transform of events in the sense organ) is then transmitted to some effector organ of the system, such as the furnace, and causes this organ to act in an appropriate sense to modify the value of the perceived variable. (When the temperature of the house falls, the furnace is activated; or when the temperature rises, the furnace is shut off.) A similar system obtains in the aiming of a rifle. The rifleman looks along the sights and observes the error of his aim at Time 1. He then moves the rifle to correct this error and observes the new value of error at Time 2, and so on, until he decides to press the trigger. The essence of the matter is that a corrective process is activated by perceived error.

In contrast to the method of feedback is the method of calibration. A man firing a shotgun at a flying bird does not depend upon a process of successive self-correction. He receives a single slug of information at Time 1 (an estimate of the bird's position, the velocity and direction of its movement). He immediately raises the gun to a position which he computes will place the shot where the bird will be at Time 2, and fires. There is not "error activation" between the moment of initially observing the bird and the moment of pressing the trigger. It is as if the marksman were calibrated to rigid mechanisms that will predictably compute in a given way. It is only in *learning* to handle a shotgun that feedback enters. The learner may observe that in a series of shots he has fired too high or too low or too soon and he may use this observed error to change his habitual calibrated response.

Note that *habit* is, in general, an economical method of solving familiar problems by the substitution of calibration for feedback.[8] The first time we meet a new problem we solve it by feedback or trial and error. Later, habit will short-cut this process.

The first question to ask about any system characterized by feedback or calibration is: Is this system stable? But to attribute "stability" to a system is to make a statement about the ongoing truth of some statement about the system. More rigorously, we

---

[8] To rely upon feedback is a common "bad habit" of beginners with the shotgun; strictly, this is perhaps a meta-habit.

117

should ask what descriptive statements about this system have ongoing truth? Within what limitations?

An organism is a system for which many statements describing process inside the system continue to be true up to the limit of death and in spite of the gradual replacement of the material of which the system is made. A social system may show stability in spite of the death and replacement of the individuals of which it is composed.

The Families of Schizophrenic Patients

We can now ask some first questions about the families containing schizophrenics. Are these systems stable? What descriptive statements about these systems have ongoing truth, despite what sorts of impact or disturbance?

1. Our observations show that these families, in a gross sense, continue as families. The statement, "This is a closely intercommunicating system," continues to be true in spite of the very considerable unhappiness of the members and even in spite of such external divisive forces as the military draft.[4]

2. These families seem to be stable with relation to the descriptive statement, "This family contains a schizophrenic." If the identified patient shows sudden improvement, the behavior of the others will change in such a way as to push him back into schizophrenic behavior. Or if the identified patient recovers, behavior in the family will change in such a way that some other family member starts to show psychological stress. He may almost invite the "normal" members of the family to treat him as the identified patient.

3. It has been noted that some of these families are stable in regard to the descriptive statements that the neighbors might make about them. In spite of gross cultural abnormality within the family circle, the family maintains stability in its external appearance and respectability. The identified patient may, and usually

___

[4] The families with which we have worked in the Palo Alto projects are, however, a specially selected sample. We insist upon the availability of both parents, and we take only families in which it is the offspring who is the identified patient. This descriptive imputation of family stability seems characteristic of this sample.

does, try to disrupt the external veneer, but the rest of the family will make strenuous efforts to defend the external appearances.

4. The families containing schizophrenics exhibit a stability that is, in general, not present in normal families. Many descriptive statements about the relationship between members remain true much longer than in usual families Indeed, these statements may be said to be stable under the impact of the processes of maturation of the independent members. The growing up of the identified patient and the senescence of the parents scarcely seem to affect the patterns of behavior between parent and offspring. Over-protectiveness, if present, continues undiminished and the incessant inconsistencies of relationship that we have called "double binds" continue unabated.

Many other statements might be made about these families and we could profitably discuss the mechanisms that determine their ongoing truth. The statements made above, however, are enough to illustrate the method of study.

Next, we have to ask whether the on-going truth of these statements is maintained by feedback or by calibration or by some *combination* of these processes. This question must, however, be delayed until the combination patterns have been briefly discussed.

Combinational Patterns

Characteristically, feedback and calibration seem to operate at alternate levels. By translating the word "stability" to mean an imputation of ongoing truth to a particular descriptive statement, I have implicitly suggested that there are levels of stability, just as there are levels of descriptive statement. In fact, these levels must necessarily be in a hierarchy of logical types and, as mentioned above, feedback and calibration seem rather commonly to be used alternately at alternate levels. For example, the thermostatic system of a house operates by feedback, but this feedback is controlled in turn by a calibrational device on the wall of the living room which can be set (calibrated) to a given temperature from which the actual temperature of the living room will vary only slightly. The dial on the wall in an inhabited house is controlled in turn by feedback mechanisms involving the sense

119

organs of the inhabitants. Somebody says, "The house is always too cold." He is "error activated" to go and change the calibrational setting of the dial which in turn will change the feedback operations of the thermostatic system.

A similar alternating hierarchy can be observed in society's attempts to control culturally deviant behavior. When certain norms or thresholds are overpassed, this deviation activates policemen or psychiatrists to go and do something about it. But the setting of these norms is, at least in some societies, achieved by a calibrational system called "the law." The setting of this system determines what shall be regarded as deviance and how far an individual may go before either policemen or psychiatrists are activated. The law itself, however, is subject to change by complex feedback mechanisms involving debate, voting, and so on. The Medes and Persians who boasted that their law "altereth not," were living under a relatively primitive system of law which antedated the luxuries and complexities of democratic automation.

We must expect that the ongoing truth of any given descriptive statement about a system will be maintained by a hierarchy of mechanisms—some of them feedback, some of them calibration. Let me recall again the fact that in human behavior there is a tendency for feedback mechanisms to be replaced gradually by the calibrational mechanisms of habit. This principle obtains even at the social level, where precedent lays a base for law; for example, cohabitation may ultimately constitute a common law marriage.

Re-examination of Statements

When re-examined in the light of these considerations, our statements about the family become classifiable as belonging to several levels, and at a higher level we have statements about the family in relation to the outside community. Statement 1, that the family continues as a closely intercommunicating system, contains mixed elements of both these levels. On the one hand the family is stable, in the sense of avoiding visible signs of disruption, such as divorce, scattering, and so on, but the statement also contains comments about closeness or interdependence as exemplified by behavior within the family constellation.

120

Statement 2, that the family contains "an identified patient," also seems to be valid on two levels. This is a statement about interpersonal behavior, but it also implies a degree of habit formation, that is, calibration, within the identified patient. To be a schizophrenic is more than merely acting schizophrenic when the occasion demands. The statement suggests that the identified individual is partly unable to drop his schizophrenic behavior in contexts where that behavior would be inappropriate; the behavior is no longer totally subject to feedback control.

Statement 3, that "external appearances" are maintained, may be seen as a statement of a calibrated law or rule for these families.

Statement 4 concerns only the interpersonal behavior and suggests certain impacts and pressures under which this behavior still remains constant—the changing stresses of maturation.

But what was said earlier about the alternating sequences of feedbacks and calibrations suggests that we ought to look for sequences of this kind as an over-all structure within which the statements to which we have imputed ongoing truth would have their place. Precisely at this point, our schizophrenic families begin to show very peculiar characteristics. The only calibrations that seem to be viable in these families are at the very low level of individual habit formation and at the highly superficial level of external appearances. Perhaps I am exaggerating, but I shall illustrate this statement by observations of one particular family.

I observed that this family regularly arrived for their family sessions between fifteen and twenty minutes late. I briefly investigated the mechanics of this regularity in the course of a conversation in which I was trying to find generalizations that could be regarded as "rules" for this family. It became evident that it was inconceivable for them to operate by a regular rule that would ensure their arrival for a family session at any specified time. The regularity of their lateness was, in fact, achieved by complex family interaction and interpersonal struggle which lasted about the same length of time every week. The father—an intermittently authoritarian character—claimed that he tried to lay down rules, but the mother acted on the premise that no rule that he laid down could have validity because she was sure he would not maintain his own rule.

There was also in this family no regular premise giving authority to any member and no regular premise governing how rules, if there were any, should be changed. The father's edicts fell to the ground not only because the mother would not let them stand, but also because he could admit no feedback correction or flexibility.

To propose a calibration in this family would be to commit an error that would immediately activate feedback processes. In sum, we have here a system that operates between the fixed points of individual habit (and no member dare change his habits) and certain premises regarding external behavior. The latter premises are under constant attack by the identified patient, who is likely to remark in a clear conversational tone in church, "We haven't had a nice crackling storm lately; have we, dad?" All between these points is feedback.

Perhaps a truly anarchic system might work with only feedback, and feedback controlling feedback, without intermediate calibration. This, at least, is the anarchist's ideal. The system described, however, is not anarchic. Habits are rigid; external appearances must be controlled, and the father continually tries to lay down inflexible rules. The result is a system which, while pathogenic, is yet stable. Many statements about it appear to have enduring truth.

You will note, however, that what I have been able to say is very inconclusive. I believe that we are today only on the threshhold of being able to ask those questions about family organization that will be both answerable by research and incisive. These questions will transcend the unique episodic detail of what happens in a given family, by relating the details to our small formal knowledge of the processes of biosocial integration.

The Need for an Epidemiology of Psychiatric Disorders of the Family

Iago Galdston

WERE I IN NEED of a poetic motto for my discourse I would select Browning's lines:

But a man's reach must exceed his grasp
Or what's a heaven for?

In this instance my reach most certainly exceeds my grasp, and I might add, that of any man, for in the true sense of the term *the epidemiology* of psychiatric disorders of the family is yet to be defined or even recognized; its import still awaits acknowledgment. In other words, there are but few who have an animating awareness of this most pertinent field of study.

This affirmation may seem a bit odd, particularly since in recent years a good deal of concern with psychiatric epidemiology [1] has been exhibited. Many so-called epidemiological studies have been conducted, many epidemiological surveys have been made, and many epidemiological conferences have been held. What merit is there, then, to my contention that the very meaning of the epidemiology of psychiatric disorders of the family remains unrecognized and undefined?

The seeming paradox, the apparent contradiction, between my affirmation and what is being done and achieved in psychiatric epidemiology derives not from my failure to appreciate the latter

[1] See *Epidemiology of Mental Disorder;* Milbank Memorial Fund Proceedings, Vol. XXVI. Papers presented at a Round Table at the 1949 Annual Conference of the Milbank Memorial Fund, November 16–17, 1949. Milbank Memorial Fund, New York, 1950.

efforts, but rather from the different sense in which I use the term "epidemiology." [2] The issue is not merely one of semantics; it is one of crucial importance. What is commonly taken to be epidemiology is, in the vast majority of instances, essentially no more than demography, that is, a *statistical* study of populations in relation to one another, or a multiple study of population factors, determinable statistically, that is, numerically or mathematically.

Definition of Terms

I have said that most of the so-called studies in psychiatric epidemiology are "no more than demography." But the "no more" is not meant to disparage. For certain purposes demography is very useful, indeed indispensable. Thus, if one is responsible for planning clinic services, or hospital facilities for the mentally ill, it is both good and necessary to know the pertinent demographic data—how many per hundred or per thousand of the general population are likely to require such services. Demography can and does provide us with many refined data concerning, for example, differentials in age, sex, race, economic status, and so on. We can and do obtain some interesting demographic data bearing on the rise or decline in the prevalence of diseases, and these data may serve to establish, qualify, or deny the value of different therapeutic or prophylactic agents and procedures, as, for example, the use of penicillin in the treatment of syphilis, or the effectiveness of the Salk vaccine in the prevention of poliomyelitis.

Demography can also tell us a good deal about the family constellation, for example, what percentage of mothers work outside the home during the day; or how frequently more than one member of a family is hospitalized because of mental illness; and so on, in respect to matters infinite in number, and limited only by the ingenuity and curiosity of the inquirer.

We see then that demography does afford us much invaluable information. Yet I must insist that demography is nothing more than demography. It is of inestimable value to epidemiology; it is not, however, epidemiology, or in any sense its equivalent. I shall not belabor this point any further save to comment that

[2] Iago Galdston, "Evaluation of This Material," *Epidemiology of Mental Disorder, op. cit*, pp. 90–92.

some of the most egregious blunders in medical history derive from the failure to differentiate clearly between the data of demography and the insights afforded by epidemiology.

But if demography is not epidemiology, what then *is* epidemiology? And in what specific sense do I use this term?

We find little to instruct us in the etymology of the word. Derived from the Greek it simply means "epi"—in or among, "demos" —the people, and "logos"—the word, to be translated freely as the knowledge of. It is not in its etymology but in its historical derivation that we can find the true meaning of epidemiology, and for this we must turn to Hippocrates, the "father of medicine." In this connection let me cite a passage from the writings of one of the most distinguished among the recent British epidemiologists. In 1930, Crookshank,[3] in the Introduction to his *Epidemiological Essays* wrote as follows:

> There is a real danger, at the present time . . . lest the Hippocratic Epidemiology, as developed by Baillou, by Sydenham, by Huxham, [and—I will add—by Creighton[4] and by Hamer[5]] be swallowed up in Statistical Science. Statistics may swallow up but can never replace Epidemiology. There is, no doubt, a statistical method of examining and appraising epidemiological data that is admirable and praiseworthy enough. But Epidemiology, the study of epidemics, has to do primarily, not with figures and numbers, but with Peoples, Times, Seasons, Airs, Waters, and Places. . . .

Let me underscore this—epidemiology has to do primarily not with figures and numbers, but with peoples, times, seasons, airs, waters, and places. In psychiatric epidemiology, airs and waters are of less import, though not entirely without significance. But peoples, times, seasons, and places are of the highest order of pertinence. It is in the perspective of these determinants that we can understand disease as dissociation of the functional unity of the organism, or the failure to attain such functional unity. In this perspective we can carry out the contemplation and study of *living man*, of man reacting to a host of influences, internal as

[3] Francis Graham Crookshank, *Epidemiological Essays*, K. Paul, Trench, Trubner and Co., London, 1930.

[4] Charles Creighton, *A History of Epidemics in Britain*, 2 vols., Cambridge University Press, London, 1891–1892.

[5] Sir William Hamer, *Epidemiology Old and New*, K. Paul, Trench, Trubner and Co., London, 1928.

well as external, and revealing his individuality in his method of reaction; not only in anatomical form but in temperament, that is functionally and psychically.

The Multiplicity of Causes

All this refined inquiry into the true meaning of epidemiology may seem tedious. I confess it to be something of a labor to expound and, I suspect, as much of a labor to attend. Yet I should like to urge that it is entirely worth the effort, for it is richly laden with significance. It may afford us a truly meaningful comprehension of disease. Let me cite in evidence a very simple illustration. We all have some knowedge of tuberculosis, and most of us, if we were asked the cause of tuberculosis, would be likely to respond "the tubercle bacillus." That is what is generally taught. The germ of tuberculosis is *the cause* of tuberculosis; the spirochete of syphilis in *the cause* of syphilis, and so on, not only in regard to the infectious diseases but in explanation of other untoward effects; that is, a given condition is the result of a specific cause, as, for example, automobile accidents result from speed and home accidents from carelessness.

But the fact is this just is not so. Few things that man experiences and few results of his actions are unifactorial in causation.[6] Into all of them enters a complex of determinants, including as Hippocrates had written, peoples, times, seasons, and places. This truth applies not less, but rather more, to psychiatric ills than to physical ills.

When I was a student in Vienna in the early twenties I came upon a series of caricatures that spoofed the medical specialists. The surgeon was represented in a blood-splattered gown, saying "Gut is' 'gangen, nix is g'schehn." * The elegant, bewhiskered gynecologist, glove in hand and boutonniere in lapel, epitomized the secret of his success in the aphorism, "Komm' den Frauen zart entgegen." ** But my favorite, striking so close to home, was

6 See Iago Galdston, "The Concept of the Specific in Medicine," *Transactions and Studies of the College of Physicians of Philadelphia*, Waverly Press, Baltimore, 1941, Vol. IX, pp. 25–34.
* "Everything went well; nothing happened."
** "Meet the ladies tenderly."

that of the psychiatrist. It was not Freud who was spoofed, but rather someone else who had a rather close resemblance to Alfred Adler. He was shown seated, and before him was a self-conscious, bewildered adolescent. The psychiatrist, so the legend read, had just asked him. "Sind Sie niemals auf den Kopf gefallen?" ***

I found the humor subtle, although of course exaggerated. What pleased me most in this caricature was that it signaled and lampooned a common fallacy: the unique traumatic event. Here was a youngster on the threshold of maturity, probably anxious about masturbation and all the multiple threats and enticements of heterosexuality. But what the psychiatrist wanted to know was whether he ever fell on his head. Is it stretching the point too far to equate with this lampooned psychiatrist the one who sums up his case in terms of a castration fear, an unresolved Oedipal complex, or (as one best-seller psychologist did) the sight of what is so euphemistically called "the primal scene?" I think not!

I, of course, do not intend to deny or to discount the pathogenic potentials of the so-called traumatic event When of an egregious magnitude it can prove totally overwhelming and disruptive. But traumatic events of this order are rare indeed, and are seldom encountered in civil psychiatric experience. The pathology the psychiatric patient presents is most commonly the end result of many-factored experiences. It is the product of a complex of determinants, including, if I may repeat, peoples, times, seasons, and places.

It is in this perspective that we can fully appreciate the crucial influences of the family and its fundamental bearing on psychiatric epidemiology. For where else in the human realm do peoples, times, seasons, and places bear so intensively and so intimately on the lives and experiences of the individual? Yet oddly enough, while we have devoted much thought and study to the individual, we have paid but little attention, in terms of psychiatric dynamics, to the family. I underscore *in terms of psychiatric dynamics,* for I am aware that in recent years the family has been studied in other respects—anthropologically, sociologically, in its economic operations, in the role functions of its respective members, and

*** "Didn't you ever fall on your head?"

127

in many other respects. These studies, however, are essentially descriptive. They do carry some psychiatric implications, but these are not nodal; they are not studies of the family "in respect to psychiatric dynamics."

Emphasis and Pathology

To complicate matters even further I shall add that we know a good deal about the family *in terms of pathologic end results*. The anamnestic recitation of the psychiatric patient is largely devoted to his family, its composition, and his experiences with, and relations to, parents, siblings, and relatives. But this is, one might say, information at second hand, filtered through and structured by a reactive individual, and viewed in all respects in his own Gestalt. Only those who have had the opportunity to treat both marriage partners and both parents and their children, each in respect to his own separate and distinctive problems, can appreciate how much the essential data may be at variance as perceived, experienced, and reported by the different related individuals. Moreover, the validated fact is that pathology can teach us only how the organism reacts to injury and insult. It can teach us little on how the organism functions *as an organism*. Pathological studies can offer clues for physiological research, but the telling information on the functioning of the organism derives essentially from physiological pursuits. I might add that epidemiology need not refer only to disease; there is also an epidemiology of health, implemented in practice by hygiene and prophylaxis.

It is undeniable that psychiatry throughout its long history has been almost entirely preoccupied with the disease states, that is, with psychopathology. Only during the past few decades has any interest been shown in normal psychophysiology. Much of it has properly centered on the psychological growth and development of the child.

Because psychiatry has been so much preoccupied with pathology, its theoretical formulations on disease causations and its reflected ideas on disease prevention have, in numerous instances, been rather bizarre. Thus, it may be recalled that Freud at one time believed that onanism resulted in the production of some toxic substance injurious to the body. Nor should Freud be singled out for this belief. Simon André Tissot ascribed to onanism all the possible evils of the body and mind.[7] And as late as 1912, Hermann Rohleder propounded the same rather malign ideas.[8] I cite these instances as examples of what I would designate as "etiological reasoning from pathology." The sequence of this reasoning is rather simple and naive. It had been observed that neurotics and psychotics were addicted to masturbation. Hence, it seemed reasonable to deduce that neuroses and psychoses resulted from excessive masturbation.

Psychiatry, it should be noted, is not the only medical specialty that is prone to reason from pathology to etiology. Such reasoning is common in all of medicine; witness the latest instance, relating cholesterol to atherosclerosis. However, academically at least, psychiatry should be the one medical specialty least liable to such inadequate and often faulty reasoning.

Importance of Family Relationships

Certainly, and at least since the time of Freud, it has been clear that psychiatric disorders (save only those patently of an organic origin) derive from the interactional experiences of persons, and notably from the interrelations of parents and their children. "In the course of his pioneer work," wrote Flügel in *The Psycho-Analytic Study of the Family*, "Freud himself had in more than one connection drawn attention to the importance of the family relationships in regard to the general development of character and vital activity of the individual." [9] The importance of the family relationships, however, has been more affirmed than explored. Flügel's own work, unique as an enterprise, is, despite its title, far less a *study* of the family than the application of psychoanalytic theory to the *explication* of the family.

[7] Simon André Tissot, *L'Onanism. Essai sur les Meladies Produites par la Masturbation*, Garnier Frères, Paris, 1874.

[8] Hermann Rohleder, *Die Masturbation, Eine Monographie für Aerzte und Pedagogen*, 3rd ed., Fischer, Berlin, 1912.

[9] J. C. Flügel, *The Psycho-Analytic Study of the Family*, 4th Edition, Hogarth Press, London, 1931, p. 32.

129

Since Freud had drawn attention to the importance of family relationships, why has this field of study been so largely neglected among psychoanalysts? The reason, I am persuaded, derives from the nature and pattern of psychoanalytic practice. In no other department of medical practice, in no other specialty, and at no time in medical history has there been the exclusive closeting of patient and doctor, analysand and analyst, that is *de rigueur* in orthodox psychoanalysis. I fully understand the rationale of that exclusiveness; it is the pattern of the religious confessional. It assures the communicant of the inviolability of the confidential nature of his communication. It also, be it noted, guarantees him the opportunity to tell *his* story without running the risk of having it checked or challenged by anyone else. It altogether facilitates free communication *from patient to analyst,* and this, particularly when the preferred, if not insisted on, pattern of communication is "free association," is deemed the sovereign process of the analytical therapeutic enterprise.

I fully understand the rationale in terms of the avowed objectives. But what of the objectives? First, however, let us consider actual practice. Among the persons related to the patient there are some who are very content, indeed happy, that the relationship between the patient and the therapist is of such a confidential and exclusive nature. Such individuals—the parents of a child, or the patient's mate—are, one might say, glad to have no part in the "case." They have done their duty; they turned "the problem" over to the experts, and it's up to the patient and his psychiatrist to get things straight. Should the therapist be so unorthodox as to want to see the "other parties," they are likely to inquire in astonishment, "Why does he want to see me?" Such individuals come—when they do come—with a sense of having been injured, and expecting not to be charged for the hour. On the other hand, there are some who are eager to see the analyst, "just to set him straight," to tell him *their* side of the story, for they are certain the analyst is being taken in. Generally, such individuals already are dubious about psychiatry and have sent their child, or consented to their mate's psychotherapy, under compulsion or duress. In my own practice, and always of course with the consent of the patient, I have in many instances welcomed

130

a visit from such "eager beavers" or "doubting Thomases" and the visit has not always turned out to be without profit for all concerned.

The most trying of experiences is to be consulted by someone who is close to and deeply involved with a patient, and who is troubled and confused and much in need of counsel and guidance, but is not able to reach the patient's therapist. I experienced such a consultation recently. The father of a sick girl, a widower, living alone with this 26-year-old daughter, was beside himself because he did not know what to do. The girl had seen, for periods ranging from several weeks to several months, no fewer than twelve psychiatrists. She was, to quote her, "in search of the right man, and hadn't found him yet." None of the analysts and therapists would see the father, or advise him how he might deal with his part in the dilemma.

Admittedly the father was a passive and masochistic character. But this fact, far from being beside the point, is very relevant to the point. How much better the analysts who had the girl in treatment might have understood the case, and the girl's search for the "right man," had they seen not only the girl but the father as well.

So much for the data of experience. Let me revert to the query, "What of the objectives?" The reference is to the objectives of psychoanalytic therapy, and it may be extended to embrace any and every order of psychoanalytically-oriented psychotherapy. What of the objectives? They are circumscribed by the reality situation, which can usually be described in this way: an individual in difficulties, the patient, engages another individual of reputed knowledge and skills, the therapist, to help him resolve and surmount his difficulties. This is not an "epidemiological situation," and the contract is not between the *demos* and the therapist, but between an individual and an individual. What I am trying to convey is that the exclusive character of the psychoanalytic relation of patient and analyst is freighted with much ritual and taboo, but even were it entirely freed of these encumbrances, it would still remain a time-and-problem-bound relationship of a contractual nature between one individual and another individual. For competent psychotherapy a broader and more intimate knowledge of the familial complex is needed than is currently appreciated or sought. But in ordinary experience, within the ordinary setting of psychiatric practice, the possibilities for gaining broad and intimate knowledge of the familial complex, so basic for psychiatric epidemiology, are limited. They are limited by the therapeutic commitment, that is by the contractual relation of patient and therapist. Yet even within these limits contact with the other components of the family complex can and should be made precisely in terms of the therapeutic goal, with the aim of thereby helping the patient to resolve and surmount the difficulties that brought him into therapy.

The full attainment of the therapeutic goal is frequently impossible without the involvement of some or most of the other members of the familial complex. Failure to achieve such involvement, either because it was not attempted or because the others refused to become involved, commonly results in only partial therapeutic success, obtained—and I must underscore this point— at the cost of alienation of the patient from the family or of the two partners. The jibe "so she went to a psychoanalyst and then divorced her husband" is not to be brushed off as pure ignorance or malice.

From all the foregoing we can perceive that, although Freud and his associates in psychoanalysis recognized the importance of the family relationship in regard to the general development of character and vital activity of the individual, neither psychoanalytic, nor psychoanalytically-oriented psychotherapy has adequately explored the nature, qualities, and dimensions of the family relationships, or is in a position to do so effectively. Yet, it is precisely the determination of the nature, qualities, and dimensions of family relationships that is quintessential to the epidemiology of psychiatric disorders of the family.

Conclusions

The objective conclusions to be drawn from these elaborated considerations can be formulated thus: Psychiatric epidemiology is to be distinguished from and differentiated from psychiatric demography. Psychiatric epidemiology is to be comprehended

132

in the Hippocratic formulation, involving the long-term, many-factored interplay of peoples, times, seasons, and places, understood in their widest meanings and deepest implications. It is within the setting of the family that these factors effect their most telling results, in health or in illness, most critically in the formative years of the individual but also throughout his life.

The interpretation of etiology in terms of the pathological end results is at best limited, and at worst misleading. The etiology, or genetic derivation, of psychopathology is better understood in the intimate perception of the long-term interplay of the epidemiological components within the familial setting.

Psychotherapy is innately limited when centered on manifest pathology. To be more fully effective it must embrace the full spectrum of the epidemiological components. This ideal desideratum is seldom attainable, but it is possible to a far greater extent than is currently appreciated or attempted.

Crucial and fundamental to an understanding of psychiatric epidemiology is the study of the epidemiology of psychiatric disorders of the family. Such study cannot be conducted during individual psychotherapy, or coincidentally with it. It requires *institutional* organization and pursuit, and calls for multidiscipline analysis, in which psychiatry is the prime commitment and the central orientation. Another and more compelling reason why the epidemiological study of the family calls for institutional pursuit is that such study must embrace the normal family as well as post-therapy normalized families.

Historically, it is pertinent to recall that most of our agencies were organized to treat the ill, not to prevent illness. As a result, they are not yet streamlined to take action on, or a real part in the solution of, those problems that create the ills they seek to alleviate. It was in this context that Stanley P. Davies expressed fond hope that "perhaps we can look forward to the day when with the help of the social scientist we can look deeply into the successful family, for example, and see what makes it tick so that other families may be helped to find and blend the same ingredients to get the same desired result." [10]

[10] Stanley P. Davies, "The Relation of Social Science to Social Welfare," *Social Work Journal*, Vol. XXXI, No. 1 (1950), p. 20.

An outstanding example of the study of family epidemiology is Sir James C. Spence's *Survey of a Thousand Families in Newcastle Upon Tyne.*[11] It is, however, devoted almost entirely to the clinical and does not include the psychiatric disorders. The aim of the Spence study was to "identify the diseases of childhood in a representative sample of families, to trace their origins and to measure their effects." The study was designed to be "primarily a clinical and epidemiological study substantiated by direct observation and immediate record." "In designing the experiment," the authors affirmed, "we decided that in no other way could we obtain the facts we sought than by an intimate and continuous study of an adequate sampling of the families in the city."

It is noteworthy that the institutionally organized and supported disciplines—anthropology, sociology, social psychiatry, economics, and social work—have been most preoccupied with "the family," while psychiatry itself has been a laggard rather than a leader. I do not wish, however, to overlook the efforts of a few pioneers in the field. Martin Grotjahn's recently published book[12] includes a chapter on the history and development of psychoanalytic family therapy in which he describes the work of some of these pioneers. Prominent among the individuals who have done pioneer work in family therapy is Dr. Nathan W. Ackerman, well known for his writings[13] on the subject and as a prime organizer of the recently established Family Institute in New York. It is to such organizations that we look for the psychiatric epidemiology that is so urgently needed.

[11] Sir James C. Spence, *Survey of a Thousand Families in Newcastle Upon Tyne,* Oxford University Press, London, 1954.
[12] Martin Grotjahn, *Psychoanalysis and the Family Neurosis,* W. W. Norton and Co., New York, 1960.
[13] See, for example, *The Psychodynamics of Family Life,* Basic Books, New York, 1958.

The Challenge of Research in Family Diagnosis and Therapy

Summary of Panel Discussion [1]

Marjorie L. Behrens

The relatively brief contributions that follow represent a fair sample of the current diversity of approach and interest in family research in the mental health field. The challenge for all is to acquire more precise knowledge of the family toward a goal of increased mental health. As we begin to probe and learn, however, we find that the complexities seem to multiply and the area of needed investigation, far from decreasing, grows larger and larger. But to the extent that the ramifications of the problem of research in family diagnosis and therapy become more clearly defined, we should feel encouraged. We begin to see more exactly with what we are dealing. Such knowledge helps us increasingly to determine an appropriate focus for specific studies, to decide on a more rational basis what we can omit, and to feel safer in the investigation of limited aspects of the family because we have more confidence about the context into which the parts may fit.

Interest in the family and family research crosses many professional lines, even when it is narrowed to family diagnosis and therapy. Within this one area, there are still many differences—in the reasons for study, in starting points, in methods, in study scope, and in the foci and levels of specificity. Our panel, which represents different disciplines (psychiatry, sociology, psychology, and anthropology) reflects all these. The impetus for the studies reported

[1] Participants in the panel were: Dr. Nathan W. Ackerman, *Chairman,* Gregory Bateson, Mrs. Marjorie L. Behrens, Dr. Leonard S. Cottrell, Jr., Dr. Don D. Jackson, Dr. Hope J. Leichter, and Dr. Henry L. Lennard.

differs and the points of view and work reported vary considerably. On some points, however, there is agreement, albeit of a negative sort. It is agreed, for example, that our language is inadequate to deal with the multiple aspects of the family and processes of inter-action; that we have too little information about normal or healthy family functioning and too little on the relationship between bio-logical and social processes. Yet, what is important is that each contributor adds to our knowledge of the family and widens our perspectives.

The range of topics discussed by the panel includes an analysis of some typical interactions in schizophrenic families, particularly in relation to "double binds"; a discussion of the importance for research of variations in family boundaries; a report on some of the difficulties facing the social scientist in this field and an attempt to quantify observable aspects of family conflict; and the problem of helping the family formulate goals and develop the "interpersonal competence" necessary to achieve them. Additional remarks by the speakers and other panel members have been summarized.

1. Formal Research in Family Structure

Gregory Bateson

It will perhaps be useful to present some of the formal consider-ations with which we have been working in Palo Alto.[2] Our task has had two main components: (1) defining and classifying those phenomena that have hitherto been lumped together under the general term "double bind"; and (2) relating these phenomena to the mechanisms of family organization in those families in which there is a schizophrenic member.

It is perhaps only the latter half of our work that is immediately relevant to this conference, but it is necessary for me to introduce

[2] The ideas in this paper emerged from research projects for the Study of Schizophrenic Communication, financed by the Foundations' Fund for Research in Psychiatry administered by Stanford University and by Grant No. OM-324 from the National Institute of Mental Health administered by the Palo Alto Medical Research Foundation. These projects are a part of the research program of the Veterans Administration Hospital, Palo Alto, California.

the problems of family organization by first outlining how we now conceive of the double bind and its varieties.

You will recall that there has long been controversy about the nature of "experimental neurosis." "Neurotic" conditions are induced in mammals of various species in a somewhat standard manner. The animal is first trained to discriminate between two stimuli, for example, an ellipse and a circle, and when this training is completed the stimuli are modified. The ellipse is inflated and the circle is flattened until the two stimuli come to resemble each other so closely that the animal cannot distinguish between them. During this process the animal, up to a point, becomes increasingly skilful in discriminating between the stimuli but finally fails to do so. At this point he develops the disturbances of behavior that have been called "experimental neurosis." These disturbances may be gross, are difficult to cure, and may persist for the remainder of the animal's life.

Various explanations of the etiology of this disturbed behavior have been offered. It has, for example, been ascribed to a breakdown of discrimination. As I see it, in the final phases of the experiment the learning context is not one that would demand that the animal make discriminations. It is a probabilistic context. Stimuli that cannot be discriminated are, for all psychological purposes, identical. The same context could therefore be constructed if the experimenter used only one stimulus object and tossed a coin to decide whether to reward or to punish in each successive trial. Correspondingly, the animal would be wise to stop trying to discriminate and, instead, simply gamble upon the outcome. Interestingly enough, a naive animal that has not been taught that this is a context for discrimination will, in fact, do this—he will simply guess—without gross psychological disturbance.

In other words, the disturbances of behavior are induced by a learning context about which a piece of false information has been communicated to the animal. He has been trained to expect that this is a context for discrimination, whereas, in fact, it is a context in which reinforcement is contingent not upon the nature of the stimulus nor upon his response, but only upon probability. In terms of double-bind theory, I would classify the disturbances in the animal's behavior as comparable, in formal etiology, to the phenomena which in man are called schizophrenia.

There are, however, a great many ways of setting up the contingencies of a context of learning. Reinforcement may be positive or negative. It may be contingent upon stimulus alone (as in typical Pavlovian experiments); it may be contingent only upon the animal's response; it may be contingent upon some combination of stimulus and response; or it may even be contingent upon the outcome of some previous context of learning.

These considerations immediately propose a classification of those interactions we call double binds. Occasionally, an interaction will proceed according to the expectation or label that has been placed upon it. X will indicate to Y that this is an instrumental context and reinforcement will take place according to this premise. All other cases, in which the preceding contextual label disagrees with the eventuality, we call double binds, and we are now working on an array of the permutations of such false labeling.

Let me illustrate what I mean by a passage from *Mary Poppins*.[3] This is a children's book about an English nanny. Mary Poppins has taken the two children to a little gingerbread shop owned by Mrs. Corry, a tiny old woman with two large, sad daughters.

"I suppose you've come for some gingerbread?"

"That's right, Mrs. Corry," said Mary Poppins politely.

"Good. Have Fannie and Annie given you any?" She looked at Jane and Michael as she said this.

"No, Mother," said Miss Fannie meekly.

"We were just going to, Mother—" began Miss Annie in a frightened whisper.

At that Mrs. Corry drew herself up to her full height and regarded her gigantic daughters furiously. Then she said in a soft, fierce, terrifying voice:

"Just going to? Oh, *indeed!* That is *very* interesting. And who, may I ask, Annie, gave you permission to give away my gingerbread—?"

"Nobody, Mother. And I didn't give it away. I only thought—"

"You only thought! That is *very* kind of you. But I will thank you not to think. *I* can do all the thinking that is necessary here!" said Mrs. Corry in her soft, terrible voice Then she burst into a harsh cackle of laughter.

"Look at her! Just look at her! Cowardy-custard! Cry-baby!" she shrieked, pointing her knotty finger at her daughter.

[3] P. L. Travers, *Mary Poppins*, Harcourt, Brace and Co., New York, 1934, p. 121.

138

Jane and Michael turned and saw a large tear coursing down Miss Annie's huge, sad face, but they did not like to say anything, for, in spite of her tininess, Mrs Corry made them feel rather small and frightened. . . .

When Mrs. Corry says, "Have Fannie and Annie given you any?" she is labeling the context as one in which to have given ginger-bread would be rewarded and to have not given gingerbread should be explained away. But in the outcome she first keeps her daugh-ters in terrified suspense and then redefines the context by her punitive attack.

With this much definition of the double bind and its varieties, let me now turn to the problem of family organization. The question is: What mechanisms, at work in these families, generate sequences of this kind over and over again?

First, I should like to point out that the experience of sequences of this kind induces an expectation of such sequences. Miss Annie already uses a frightened whisper even before the trap is sprung. Conversely, if we think of Mrs. Corry not as the "experimenter" but as the learning subject, we note that she is rewarded by the success of her gambit. In this particular instance the reward would appear to be sadistic, but in many cases it is no more than an affirmation of *control*.

When we look at our schizophrenic families to determine the location of control in the system, we find something very peculiar —that control and responsibility are not located in the same person. In the particular family I have studied intensively, the mother would press the father to act. She told him that he should go to the son's school and make arrangements with the school officials. He did not act when pressed by her, so she finally took the initiative and went to talk to the school officials. They trembled like Miss Annie and Miss Fannie when she appeared, and the outcome of her conversations with them was often not satisfactory. She was not to blame for this unsatisfactory result, however, because her hus-band ought to have taken the initiative in the first place. Although she had taken the initiative, she did not accept the responsibility. Occasionally the husband would decide to act. He announced one day at breakfast that he was going to do something that she had been pressing him to do for some weeks and with which he did not agree. She said, "You're only doing that to please Mr. Bateson." He then said, "Well, I didn't agree with it anyway, and if I'm not going to get any credit for it I won't do it." This left the mother holding the bag.

The system of rewards and punishments is also interesting. The 17-year-old schizophrenic son had two important treats in the week. On Sunday he went to church with his father and on Friday he went to a teen-age dance club which was a treat arranged for him by his mother. When he offended his mother, she punished him by saying he could not go to church; when he offended his father, he was forbidden to go to the teen club. His mother would say that going to the club was *so* good for him, and she would then comfort him by taking him to the movies that night.

From this brief discussion, one can get some idea of the complex contradictions generated in these families in the contexts of learning and in the labeling of these contexts.

Comment

Dr. Ackerman pointed out the need to remember that, with respect to the human qualities of the individual and the family, in large part what is biological is also social, and what is social is also biological.

II. Boundaries of the Family as an Empirical and Theoretical Unit

Hope J. Leichter

I should like to raise what seems to me to be a basic question in all family research and treatment: What are the boundaries of the family as a unit? There are two parts to this question: (1) who is included in the family as an empirical unit; and (2) what are the boundaries of the family as a theoretical unit or system?

On the empirical level, the question of the social definition of who is included in the family is not simple. We tend to think of the nuclear family of husband, wife, and children as *the* family, but in doing so we are imposing a particular cultural view. From comparative studies of kinship it is clear that the definition of who is included within a family or kinship group varies considerably from one society to another. For example, the traditional Chinese extended family household included in some cases the husband's father and mother, and the husband's brothers and their wives and children. Even within our society, household composition varies considerably in different subgroups. Recent studies of urban kinship indicate that, in many groups, the nuclear family actually lives in the same household with, or has contact with, relatives more frequently than had been supposed; and that although the nuclear family may be the desired household unit, it is often not the actual one.

The individuals included in the family as a unit of study may also vary, depending on the definition of the family that is used. A household unit may, for many purposes, be the most meaningful social unit, but often it is not composed merely of husband, wife, and children. If one uses a biological definition of the family, those who are biologically related may not be socially defined as the family unit. Recent anthropological studies have indicated that the nuclear family as a recognizable social unit may not, as previously supposed, be universal.[4] Within our own society, separation, divorce, remarriage, and adoption all may mean that social and biological definitions of the family do not coincide. If the family is defined in terms of close social relationships within a group considered kin, this also may not be a household group.

When time perspectives are introduced, there is further variability in the family unit, since the group defined as the family shifts constantly throughout the family life cycle.

[4] George Peter Murdock, "Evolution in Social Organization," in *Evolution and Anthropology: A Centennial Appraisal* (Betty J. Meggers, ed.), The Anthropological Society of Washington, Washington, D. C., 1959, p 140, states: "I must also acknowledge the actual occurrence of particular developments of which I had previously doubted the possibility. One is the disappearance of the nuclear family as a significant functional unit, which has happened through the adoption of duolocal residence in a handful of societies in our sample, notably the Minangkabau (P. E. de Josselin de Jong, *Minangkabau and Negri Sembilan*, The Hague, 1952) and the Nayar caste of the Kerala (E. K. Gough, *The Traditional Kinship System of the Nayars of Malabar*. Cambridge, 1954)."

141

In a study jointly sponsored by the Russell Sage Foundation and the Jewish Family Service,[5] we are focusing on the relationships between the nuclear family and kin outside the nuclear family. The problem of defining the boundaries of the family was one factor that led us to this focus. In the early stages of the research we were examining changes in family role organization at certain transitions in the family life cycle. In our initial family interviews with clients of the Jewish Family Service, we found that in many instances the household included more than husband, wife, and children. For example, combined households that included the wife's family were common. Even when the nuclear family was a separate household unit, there were many cases in which current relationships with kin were so important in the life of the family that it was essential to learn more about relationships with kin in order to develop an understanding of role organization within the nuclear family. For example, in attempting to understand authority and control mechanisms within the nuclear family, it does not make sense to consider only husband, wife, and children in a case where the wife's mother lives in the household and takes an active part in child care and household decisions.

This variability in the family unit raises problems in conceptualizing the family as a system. Since family composition may vary greatly in age, sex, generation, and size, depending on the definition of who is included in the family unit, the difficulties of approaching the family as a system by starting with dyads and working to triads are multiplied. The study of dyadic and triadic relationships is extremely important. But since the composition of the family is highly variable, it is also important to study characteristics that are properties of the group as such, not of its component parts. The study of how certain family functions, such as household management and child care, are carried out is important since this is an approach to properties of the family as a group.

When the family is considered as a theoretical unit there are additional problems. Whatever the group that is socially defined as the family, it is in one sense an empirical, and not a theoretical,

[5] Members of the staff of the project, Studies in Family Interaction, have included: Joanne Cammett, Fred Davis, Judith Lieb, Alice Liu, William Mitchell, Candace Rogers, and Dianna Tendler. I am grateful to Judith Lieb, William Mitchell, and Candace Rogers for helpful suggestions for this paper.

142

unit. It is a unit comparable to the individual, which is, after all, not the unit in most psychological analysis—rather the unit is a concept or group of concepts about individual organization and process, such as "personality" or "defense mechanisms." Although the family is and has long been an important unit of research, there is a risk if we stop at this point and assume that the empirical unit of the family is necessarily a theoretically meaningful unit.

There are no ready answers to the problem of how the family may be conceptualized as a theoretically meaningful unit. But it should be of help to realize that the family unit may shift according to the purpose of analysis. One focus may be the relationships within the family. Another approach, implicit in much family research, is to determine how the family affects its members or what kinds of products the family turns out for society. The family alone may not be the most meaningful unit for understanding how certain types of behavior develop in family members. In the study of delinquency, for example, current knowledge would indicate that one should include individuals outside the family, that is, peer groups of family members, as well as the non-familial roles of family members. If one attempts to understand many types of individual action and family relationships only in terms of the family, one is relying on an oversimplified "single-factor" type of explanation. In our research, for example, we have indications that bonds of solidarity or coalitions within the family are vitally influenced by relationships with kin outside the nuclear family as well as by occupational contacts of family members and by friendship ties.

For many purposes, therefore, it is more useful to conceive of the family as an open, than as a closed, system. In addition, it is important to re-examine constantly what the most meaningful boundaries of the family may be for any particular purpose, and to expect that the empirical and theoretical boundaries of the family may vary considerably. Goode has said:

The accepted subfields of any science may not, at an early stage of development, be defined by the theoretically most powerful and efficient groupings of its variables, which may therefore fail to yield the most fruitful subsystems. A half century from now, when the important variables in sociology will be more precisely known, our very concrete subfields such as "family," "criminology," and "stratification," may have disappeared, to be replaced by subfields made up of quite different variables, such as "cohesion," "authority" and

143

"system maintenance" That is, when we deal with the family as one sub-system, we may simply be trying to relate the wrong variables to one another.[6]

Comment

Professor Bateson raised the problem of temporal boundaries of the family in addition to those posed by Dr. Leichter. He felt that we know almost nothing about human ethology (as contrasted to animal studies) although the processes involved in developing and delineating a family are fundamentally ethological in nature. For example, we know nothing about courtship and the complex exchanges in this process which the ethologists would call "persuasion." He suggests that double binding, either mutual or one-sided, is to be found in courtship—a profound shift in the relationship between two persons, an attempt to change both the mental and affective orientation of those concerned. If this is so, then the hypertrophy of double binding in schizophrenic families in which parents have been married as long as twenty years may well be some pathological travesty of courtship—a compulsive attempt to solve some problem that was unsolved when the couple first came together. It is as if the basic premise of marriage, "we are partners," had never been accepted. With this ethological incompleteness, go other ethological distortions. The mother seems to be dedicated to the project of trying to wean her husband. She shows no pity because pity would be inappropriate in the weaning process. But the result of her efforts is to diminish his self-confidence and increase his pathological dependence on her. Vis-à-vis the child, however, there is no weaning. The children in these families, characteristically, retain baby nicknames until they are adult.

Comment

Dr. Leichter amplified the question of time dimension raised by Professor Bateson. She pointed out that there are differences in family structure, family boundaries, and family functions at different points in the family life cycle. Diagnosis and therapy of the family require different norms for healthy relationships at different stages.

[6] William J. Goode, "Sociology of the Family," in *Sociology Today*, Robert K. Merton, Leonard Broom, and Leonard S. Cottrell, Jr. (eds.), Basic Books, New York, 1959, p 185.

III. Analysis of Family Conflict [7]

Henry L. Lennard

The social scientist engaged in research on family dynamics in relation to the development of emotional illness and on the process of therapy is in a serious dilemma. On the one hand, he believes that the social sciences today are in the same position as were the physical sciences in the late 17th century; that many hundreds of thousands of man hours of research are needed to achieve a basic understanding of interpersonal and therapeutic influence processes.

On the other hand, practitioners do and must proceed in the present. In order to carry out their work, they perhaps have to overestimate the extent of established knowledge about human behavior. To be useful, however, the social scientist must not succumb to the temptation of pretending to be farther along than he is.

What are the long-range goals of the social scientist engaged in research on the family in relation to the development of emotional disturbances? First, he would want to have available concepts and methods by which to describe and analyze the dynamics of family interaction process both longitudinally and cross-sectionally. Second, supplied with these concepts and methods, he would then study a sample of families located differently in the social structure —families encompassing a range of educational, socioeconomic, ethnic, and other statuses. It is his expectation that, as a result of delineating the characteristic attributes of communication and socialization processes in a great many families of diverse backgrounds, he will be able to document the significance of particular social processes in the evolution of healthy, as well as disturbed, psychic and emotional functioning.

Within this broad perspective one would then raise questions about many of the imaginative hypotheses currently advanced. For example, with regard to the intriguing double-bind hypothesis of Bateson and his co-workers, one would need to know how parental communications having a double-bind character are dis-

[7] Helen C. Meyers, M D. and Stephen Kempster, M.D. participated in the development of the ideas presented in this paper.

tributed in diverse social groups. Such information would help in determining the specificity of such communication patterns for families with a psychotic member.

An epidemiology of mental illness that uses the individual as the "case" will prove to be inadequate. Similarly, a study of a few families of a particular group—no matter how intensive and dynamically oriented—cannot resolve questions of specificity. What will be required in the future will be "a depth epidemiology of family communication"

Yet, such a large-scale epidemiological study of family behavior cannot be undertaken until concepts and methods for the study of particular families have been developed.

We do not have methods of study, nor the vocabulary, by which we can describe, at any one point in time, the processes that go on between family members. In a family of five, one would have to be able to describe ten interpersonal relationships; with the addition of a therapist, it would be fifteen. But any interaction between two family members affects the nature of their response to one or more other family members. Hence, we need methods of study and a language for triadic systems as well.

Furthermore, the term "interaction" does not refer to a unitary phenomenon, but involves a variety of communications between people ranging from meaningful verbal communication to body movement, posture, and so on, and their combinations.

In addition, we must decide on the unit of our study. Shall we focus on one second, one minute, one hour, or one month in the life of a family? How representative of the recurrent interaction processes in a family is any one sample of process we choose? Is this the kind of unit on which different observers with different orientations can reach a consensus? For example, in one small study we found that a team of psychiatrists and a social scientist could categorize with reliability 30-second intervals of films of family interaction in terms of six categories, but that they could not work with longer sequences.

What factors then should be studied in family interaction process? Here we get into difficulty. We all have had the experience in research that when we emphasize the verbal aspect someone will say that body movement is more important; or that when we study second by second changes, we are told that longer lasting sequences are more important; or that when we study the interaction process, it is the psychodynamic content that counts; or that when we study the present, we should really be looking at the past or vice versa. The magnitude of the problem is such that at the present stage of development it is impossible to develop concepts and methods for the study of everything at once.

Yet one may entertain a contrary hypothesis; that in family interaction process, as in biological processes, there is a great deal of redundancy and continuity; that the picture of the family that emerges from a study of interaction process indeed resembles that emerging when psychodynamic content is the emphasis; that studying the family in the present yields information similar to that yielded by a reconstruction of the family's past interrelations. In our study of a limited segment of family behavior, we found some support for this hypothesis. In this family current disagreements and conflicts reflect past disagreements. Family members, for instance, interrupt each other in a therapy session in order to report on past family conflict. Current interaction perhaps recapitulates past interaction, to paraphrase a biological proposition. In any case, this is a hypothesis worth investigating.

What one would want to be able to do, ultimately, is to study family processes on a level relevant to the problems with which we are concerned. In some current work the problem of defining relevant behavior is dealt with in terms of one problem area which interests us—quantifying manifestations of intrafamily conflict; for instance, the extent of agreement and disagreement present. Our purpose is to be able to compare families in these terms and then subsequently to relate the family's ranking on disagreement to clinical criteria. As a start we decided to limit ourselves to overt, current agreement and disagreement of one kind. Combining a notion of Haley's (of Bateson's group) with one of Bales's, we began by viewing interaction process as having a *forward movement and momentum*. We see it somewhat analogous to the trajectory of an object which, once released, would maintain a definite course unless interfered with. Similarly, if a topic is introduced by one family member, and other family members follow up on this topic or show through body posture connoting interest and attention that they permit or approve of the discussion of this topic, then the family would ordinarily continue in the pursuit of this topic unless someone introduced another topic or in other ways deflected or terminated the discussion of this subject.

The same applies to an item of non-linguistic behavior introduced by a family member. When another family member reacts to it and permits it, such behavior receives the mark of relevance. In the pilot study referred to, we categorize the behavior of every family member—for 30-second intervals—on the basis of a sound film in a number of ways *only* with reference to whether he *overtly* accepts or rejects the topic introduced. (He may differ with regard to attitude or value about the ideas introduced; as long as he converses about the topic, he does not deflect the conversational or behavioral trajectory. There may be agreement by son and mother to talk about father though the son may praise him and the mother attack him.)

With this emphasis, then, the range of behavior that has to be observed and classified is limited immediately. A great number of intrapsychic states may be expressed through body movement or facial expression by members of the family. As long as such communications have *no direct and immediate* bearing on the direction of the interaction process, they need not concern us for purposes of observation. To an extent, many communications coming from one family member are not perceived by another family member; as long as their threshold does not exceed a certain intensity, such messages may not determine the outcome we are trying to assess.

To illustrate our categories: *Active agreement* to let one family member "carry the ball" (initiate and pursue a topic or theme) is manifested by a family member's verbal response to or verbal continuation of a topic introduced by the other, by posture such as moving forward in a chair toward the person talking, or facial movements of smiling, nodding, looking at the person talking, and so on.

Coding three and a half minutes of a family of four interacting with a therapist shows interesting sequences. (See Figure I, next page).

148

F—Father
M—Mother
S—Son
D—Daughter
T—Therapist

FIGURE I

DIRECTION OF INTERACTION PROCESS

(3½ minute sample of a family interview)

Topical Reference Intra-Personal or Inter-Personal	Person(s) Talking	Who Initiates	Theme	Agreement Active	Agreement Tacit	Disagreement Active	Disagreement Tacit	Agreement or Disagreement Not Determinable	Who Objects to Person(s) Talking
F	T,F	T responds to F		T,F	M,S			D	
S,F	S,T	T responds to S		T,F,S	M,D				S
M,F	F,S,T	T responds to F		F,M	D			S	M
S,F	S	T		S	S	M		D	M
M	M	M		F		S		D,T	
M	M,T	M		T	F		S	D	
M	M,T,F	M		T,F			S	D	
M	M,T	M			F,T		S	D	
M	M,T	M		T,F			S,D		

We can see that when the topic is introduced by the therapist or the father and deals with the father, the son usually supports the continuation of the topic. When the mother takes over the conversational initiative and talks about herself, the son through body posture shows disagreement about the direction of the conversation. The therapist initiates topics in response to bits of nonverbal behavior (father sighs) while family members respond more to verbal cues. Apparently, the intensity of a communicational stimulus that elicits a therapist's response can be lower than for family members.

The sample of family interaction here coded is from a family that has been studied intensively by a team of psychiatrists. Scoring family conflict about conversational direction for this family yields some of the major axes of family conflict as do extensive psychodynamic write-ups of the family. To the extent that such a brief interactional analysis can rank this family in comparison with others, it becomes useful. One may, as a start, limit the kinds of family communications one observes and scores, in accordance with the goals of the research. One cannot, of course, stop with the categories described here.

In conclusion, let me mention additional implications of the gap between what we know and can measure, and the needs of the practitioner. Since he is not applying a confirmed body of knowledge as does the engineer or the surgeon, he must be aware of the tentative and hypothetical character of everything he does. In a sense he is continuously testing concepts and hypotheses. Yet the experience of each practitioner is of necessity a limited one. How does he learn from the experiences of his colleagues? How does knowledge become additive? One way certainly is through the collection of objective data on family interaction through films, through tape recordings, and through interviews with family members. A second way is through reporting his experience to his colleagues descriptively and less theoretically, and a third is through his willingness to change and revise his concepts as more basic information is gathered on interpersonal and therapeutic processes.

150

IV. Interpersonal Competence and Preventive Mental Health

Leonard S Cottrell, Jr.

We need to look at the basic thought forms with which we approach this problem of the challenge of research in family dynamics. We need to go beyond diagnosis, therapy, and adjustment to planning the development of positive competence in interpersonal relations.

I was tremendously stimulated by the interest at Jewish Family Service in going beyond treatment of the intrapsychic dynamics of the individual to look at this problem in a context of interactive parts—within small and large families and in kinship groups. In other words, the matrix that comes within the purview of the diagnostician is broadened so that the problems the case presents can be seen in a larger context. But this stimulation did not stop with the notion that what we need to do is to increase our power of diagnosis and power of treatment by taking into account in a more sophisticated way the cultural and social system and the interpersonal and interactive contexts in which diagnosis and treatment can take place. This is certainly a great departure when one looks at the current orientation of the total field of the helping professions.

My imagination has carried me further in this direction—even beyond Mrs. Beatman's bold assertion that agencies dealing with people and their problems now need to go beyond treatment of the present illnesses, aches and pains, and think in terms of preventive work.[8] I should like to call your attention to the fact that treatment is still in what I call the medical model or thought form. That is to say, you assume you have a sick person or a sick group in the psychic or physical sense and you deal with that problem. If you move in the direction of prevention, it is with the notion that families need to be armed against the hazards and the illnesses that may occur—a gigantic task of bridging generational and cultural gaps, of adapting the group's behavior and goals, and its implementation of these goals in a complex and changing environ-

[8] See p. 83 of this volume.

also we must teach the organism the skills for maintaining health, the capacities to interact effectively with others.

Dr. Jackson also emphasized the need for development of a language; the language of psychiatry does not include much about health or the kind of dimensions mentioned by Dr. Cottrell. One possible new language might derive from mathematical theory and the new computers. Future research will concern itself with the more old-fashioned terms, such as compromise, collaboration, and co-operation. He noted that his research group, like Dr. Lennard's, is studying patterns of coalition. He has found a difference between apparently normal and sick families in relation to goal orientation. The apparently normal families are goal-oriented and go about achieving the goal in a direct manner, very much in contrast to the sicker families.

Mrs. Behrens emphasized some basic needs in family research in the light of present technical and conceptual limitations. She urged economy and compromise—commitment to a limited number of variables related to a specific focus. Our energies should not be diverted by a premature or perhaps impossible effort to be "scientifically" precise, but at the same time, we should make an effort to be systematic and exact whenever we can. We must face the fact that sometimes this is impossible. She mentioned several areas that need emphasis in future research: aspects of healthy functioning and their interplay with the pathological, in relation to the demands of society, and the extent to which such behavior is structured from the outside; family therapy—what the therapist does, why and how the family changes; and, finally, cutting across all these, more precise definition of clinical thinking and judgments and the variables that are clinically salient.

Index

A

ACKERMAN, Nathan W., A Dynamic Frame for the Clinical Approach to Family Conflict, 52, 17, 21, 35, 36, 38, 39, 73, 93, 134, 153
Acting out, 57, 102–103
Adaptation of family, 59
Adler, Alfred, 127
Alignments: family, 22; of father and daughter, 106; and splits, study of, 95–115; *see also* Competition and co-operation
American Orthopsychiatric Association, 40
American Psychiatric Association, 40
Analysis of Family Conflict (Lennard), 145
Anamnesis, its distortions, 128

B

Balance of family, *see* Homeostasis
Bales, Robert F., 35, 44, 67
BATESON, Gregory, The Biosocial Integration of Behavior in the Schizophrenic Family, 116, Formal Research in Family Structure, 136; 39, 40, 144, 152
Beaglehole, Ernest, 38
BEATMAN, Frances L., Trends Toward Preventive Practice in Family Service, 83; 151
BEHRENS, Marjorie L., Summary of Panel Discussion, 135; 154
Bell, Norman W., 36
Benedict, Ruth, 6
Biology of family behavior, 7–10
Biosocial Integration of Behavior in the Schizophrenic Family, The (Bateson), 116
Biosocial Unity of the Family, The (LaBarre), 5
Black case: boundaries of family, 23–24; complementarity, 23–25; psychosocial unity, 26
Bleuler, Eugen, 41

Bleuler, Manfred, 41, 42
Boehm, Werner W., 15
Bóok, J. A., 42
Boundaries of the family as an Empirical and Theoretical Unit (Leichter), 140
Boundaries of family: temporal, 144; as theoretical unit, 142–144; as treatment unit, 23–24, 29, 62
Bowen, Murray, 40
Brown, George W., 35

C

Calibration, 116–122
Casework Approach to Disturbed Families, A (Mitchell), 68
Challenge of Research in Family Diagnosis and Therapy, The, 135–154
Character disorders, 75
"Check-up" in mental health, 90
Child analysis, limitations of, 33–34
Child guidance, 32, 39
Clausen, John A., 45
Clinical social science, 21, 35, 44–45
Coding interactions, 148–149
Collaborative individual therapies of family members, 30
Collective denial, 63
Communication, non-verbal, 64, 148
Communication theory, 39, 40, 147–148
Community Service Society of New York, 17
Competition and co-operation, 54–55
Complementarity in roles, 22, 23–25, 53–54, 57, 59, 66
Concept of the Family in Casework Theory, The (Sherman), 14
Concurrent family and individual therapy, 30
Conflict, control of, in family relations, 52–56; *see also* Competition and co-operation, Family role, Social role theory
Conjoint family therapy, 29, 36, 37, 41–42; *see also* Family group therapy, Family group therapy session, Role of family therapist

Co-operation, *see* Competition and co-operation
COTTRELL, Leonard S, Jr., Inter-personal Competence and Preventive Mental Health, 151, 44
Council on Social Work Education Curriculum Study, 14
Counseling in casework, 69
Crookshank, Francis Graham, 125
Cultural adaptation, 7
Cultural matrix in family, 10–13
Cultural patterns, 45
Cultural relativity, 5–7
Culture and identity, 53
Culture and mental disorder, 38–39

D

Davies, Stanley P., 133
Defenses of family, 57
Delinquency, parental pathology in, 75
Demography: in psychiatry, 124; of schizophrenia, 42
Diagnosis, family, 29–51; 59–60, 72–74, 101–103
Disturbed families, casework approach to, 68–82, 84–85
Double bind· classification of, 136–140, 145; in courtship, 144, illustrations, 138–140

E

Eclecticism in casework, 69–70
Ego psychology, 18, 33
Epidemiology. defined, 125; of health, 128; of psychiatric disorders, 125–134
Equilibrium of family, *see* Homestasis
Etiology of pathology, 126–128
Experimental neurosis, 137
Exploratory family therapy, study of alignments and splits, 95–115, *see also* Conjoint family therapy, Family group therapy, Family group therapy session
Extended kin relations, 25, 142

F

"Fads" in mental hygiene, 92
Family, casework in, 68–82

Family diagnosis, *see* Diagnosis
Family group therapy: acting out be-tween sessions, 102–103; case illus-trations of, 23–26, 78–79, 81, 97–98, 104–113; silent members, 104, who is included, 62, 101–102, *see also* Boundaries of family, Conjoint fam-ily therapy, Role of family therapist
Family group therapy session. absences from, 102, emotional immediacy within, 62–63, 74; multiple demands of, 31, 75, 76, pair conflicts within, 74; professional preparation for, 75
"Family-healer," 57, 66; *see also* Rescue operations
Family life check-up, 90–91, 93–94
Family life cycle, 59, 90
Family life education, 86–87
Family Mental Health Clinic, *see* Jew-ish Family Service of New York
Family orientation, 18, 31
Family role. adaptations to, 53–54, changes in, through therapy, 68, 72, 79; concept, 95, *see also* Comple-mentarity in roles, Conflict, Social role theory
Father, role of, 32
Federn, Paul, 34
Feedback, application of theory to schizophrenic family, 116–122
Films of family therapy, 66, their anal-ysis, 146
Fixations in family growth, 61
Flesch, Regina, 20
Flügel, J. C, 32, 36, 129
Foote, Nelson, 44, 152
Freud, Sigmund, 33, 37, 129, 132
Fromm-Reichmann, Frieda, 34
Functions of the family, 53

G

GALDSTON, Iago, The Need for an Epidemiology of Psychiatric Dis-orders of the Family, 123
Game theory, 46
Goal-directedness in families, 46
Gomberg, M. Robert, vii, 14, 15, 19, 69, 73, 89
Goode, William J., 143
Grotjahn, Martin, 134
Group for the Advancement of Psy-chiatry, Committee on the Family, 40

H

Hallowell, A. Irving, 38
Hamilton, Gordon, 16
Hans case, 33
Healthy family, 53, 59, 90–91, 145
Hill, Reuben, 45
Hollingshead, August B., 45
Homeostasis of family group, 21–22, 40, 46, 58–59, 96
Hospitalized schizophrenic, 38, 39, see also Schizophrenic family, Schizophrenic family member

I

Identity of family, 53
Individual in the family, 20–21, 30, 58, 60, 72, 73, 130–132
Individual focus in casework, 20
Interaction in group psychotherapy, 38
Interaction process, direction of, 149
Interpersonal Competence and Preventive Mental Health (Cottrell), 151
Interpersonal and intrapersonal conflict, 27–28, 57

J

JACKSON, Don D. (and Satir), A Review of Psychiatric Developments in Family Diagnosis and Therapy, 29, 21, 39, 40, 154
Jahoda, Marie, 34
Jewish Board of Guardians, 45
Jewish Family Service of New York, 17, 25, 36, 60, 66, 134, 141, 151, 153
Josselyn, Irene M., 22

K

Kanner, Leo, 42
Kardiner, Abram, 39
Kasinin, Jacob, 38
Kaufman, Irving, 75
Kluckhohn, Florence R., 40, 45
Kraines, Samuel S., 39
Kohn, Melvin L., 45

L

LABARRE, Weston, The Biosocial Unity of the Family, 5; 26
Language, 10–11
Lasswell, Harold D., 47
Learning context, 137–138
LEICHTER, Hope J., Boundaries of the Family as an Empirical and Theoretical Unit, 140, 25, 144
LENNARD, Henry L., Analysis of Family Conflict, 145, 153
Lewin, Kurt, 21
Lidz, Theodore, 40, 42
Little case, 104–113
Longitudinal study of the family, 22

M

McGill University, 45
Main, Dr. Thomas, 104n
Malinowski, Bronislav, 7
Mammalian traits in humans, 8–10
Marital relationship, 20, 23–25, 112–113
Mary Poppins, case illustration, 138–139
Mass media in family life education, 87–88
Maudsley Hospital, 35
Mental health and illness, 34
Mental Research Institute of Palo Alto, 29, 36, 46
Merton, Robert K., 26
Meyer, Adolph, 41
Midelfort, Christian F., 40
MITCHELL, Celia, A Casework Approach to Disturbed Families, 68
Mittelmann, Bela, 33
Monadic concepts in psychotherapy, 36
Monroe, Russell R., 17
Morality, family as base of, 11–13, 84
Moreno, Jacob L., 38

N

National Institute of Mental Health, Family Studies program of, 99
Need for an Epidemiology of Psychiatric Disorders of the Family, A (Galdston), 123
New Orleans Family Service, 17

O

Oberndorf, Clarence, 33
Organismic theory of personality, 18–19
Overemphasis on pathology, 128–129

P

Palo Alto: Mental Research Institute, 29, 36, 46, Veterans Administration Hospital, 116n, 136n
Parsons, Talcott, 33, 35, 44
Pathogenic privacy, 63
Pavlovian experiments, 138
Penrose, Lionel S , 39
Philadelphia Family Society, 17
Pittsburgh family agency, 17
Pollak, Otto, 17, 45, 76
Pollock, Horatio M., 39
Positive mental health, 152
Preventive services in family agency, 83–94, 151–153
Probabilistic context for learning, 137–138
Pseudo-hostility, 110–111
Pseudo-mutuality, 108–110
Psychoanalysis, contributions of, 32–34; disagreement within, 43–44, neglect of family theory by, 130
Psychosocial dichotomy, problem of, 15–18
Psychotherapy of schizophrenia, 34–35
Public family health program, 89

R

Reality testing, 62
Redlich, Frederick C., 45
Regensburg, Jeanette, 16
Reichard, Suzanne, 39
Reiner, Beatrice Simcox, 75
Rescue operations, 112, see also "family healer"
Review of Psychiatric Developments in Family Diagnosis and Therapy (Jackson and Satir), 29
Richardson, Henry B., 39, 44
Richmond, Mary E., 27–28
Rohleder, Hermann, 129

Role of family therapist: his aims, 65–66, in appraisal, 64–65; as catalyst, 63, 77; as control, 79, functions of 61–64, 103–104; with scapegoating, 64; see also Conjoint family therapy, Family group therapy session
Rosenbaum, Peter, 105
Rudin, E , 37
Ruesch, Jurgen, 39
Russell Sage Foundation, 141, 153

S

Sacks, Patricia, 20
SATIR, Virginia (and Jackson), A Review of Psychiatric Developments in Family Diagnosis and Therapy, 29
Scapegoating, 57, 64, 80, 81, 112; case illustration of, 81–82
Schaffer, Leslie, 108
Scherz, Frances, 27
Schizophrenia: secondary symptoms, 41, therapy of, 34–35
Schizophrenic family. case illustration, 104–113; comparison with normal family, 46–47, 114, 118; literature on, 39–40; rigidity of, 118–119; rules of behavior in, 46–47, see also Hospitalized schizophrenic
Schizophrenic family member, 34–35, 37, 38
Schreber case, 37
Schwartz, Morris S., 39
Sexual acting out, 23
Sheffield, Ada, 19
Sheppard and Enoch Pratt Hospital, 88
Sherman, Irene C., 39
SHERMAN, Sanford N., The Concept of the Family in Casework Therapy, 14
Sobel, Raymond, 39
Social casework history, 15
Social institutions, 11–12
Social role theory, 14, 26–28, 71; see also Complementarity, Conflict, Family role
Social science contribution. to casework, 21, 70–71; to family diagnosis, 44–45; to psychiatry, 31–32
Social system, family as, 18, 25–26, 95, 143
Socialization of family members, 18, 53

Socio-economic influences, 45
Spence, Sir James C., 134
Spiegel, John P, 36, 40, 45
Splits and alignments· chaotic character of, 108; control of, 139; between father and daughter, 107, between parents, 106, patterns in, 54, 81, in rewards and punishments, 140, in schizophrenic family, 139, study of, 95–115
Stanton, Alfred H, 39
Study of Intrafamilial Alignments and Splits in Exploratory Family Therapy, The (Wynne), 95
Sullivan, Harry Stack, 34, 38, 42
Summary of Panel Discussion (Behrens), 135

T

Tape recordings, 104, 150
Terminological limitations in family theory, 17, 31, 43, 136, 153–154
Three-generation theory, 46, 58
Tillman, Carl, 39
Tissot, Simon André, 129
Transference, 68
Travers, P L., 138
Trends Toward Preventive Practice in Family Service Agencies (Beatman), 83

Trobrianders, 7–8
Typology of families, 21, 22, 60, 75

U

Uniqueness of family, 8–11
Universality of family, 7–8, 26
University of Minnesota, 45

V

Values, 11–13, 26–27, 76–77, 83–84
Veterans Administration Hospital, Palo Alto, 136n

W

Wahl, Charles W., 89–40
Waite, Florence T, 19
Weakland, John H., 39
Weiss, Viola, 17
Westley, William A., 45
WYNNE, Lyman C., Alignments and Splits in the Therapy of Families of Schizophrenics, 95; 41

Z

Zimbalist, Sidney E., 19

CPSIA information can be obtained
at www.ICGtesting.com
Printed in the USA
LVHW081733181119
637701LV00018B/1302/P

9 781296 615239